WITHSTANDING THE LIE

WITHSTANDING THE LIE

Roger L. Brewer and Nicole Brewer

REVISED EDITION 2016
Copyright 2016 Roger L. Brewer and Nicole Brewer

ISBN-10: 1533306567
ISBN-13: 9781533306562

R L Brewer Publications, P.O. Box 26, Rockfall, Connecticut 06481

This book is about protecting yourself from loss of self-esteem and other mental and emotional harm caused by bigotry, prejudice, discrimination, bullying, and other forms of disrespect as you await the day when everyone is treated with dignity and respect.

You can protect yourself whether the bigotry or other disparate treatment against you is based on gender, race, religion, sexual orientation, national origin, economic status, physical appearance, physical ability, job, occupation, or any other role or identity that may pertain to you.

CONTENTS

PREFACE

OUR BOOK CONTAINS two introductions (one by each of us) that provide basic information about ourselves and our motivation to do the important work we discuss in the book. Following the introductions, the book is broken into two parts. In part 1 we use ten short stories to place the vital principles, practices, and possibilities of the strategy we recommend into different settings. We believe illustration plays a critical role in conveying much of our message. In part 2 we explain the principles, perspectives, and practices of the recommended strategy, in essay form.

Some may prefer the creative interpretation in part 1. Others may prefer the direct presentation of part 2. However, we do not offer the two parts for you to choose one or the other. Instead, the two parts complement each other and are of equal importance. The book is like a road map in which the short stories provide direction and the essays describe the specific route and destination. Our hope is to give you a good understanding and a clear perspective of our message.

INTRODUCTION

By Nicole

HE HAD BLOND hair and wore his white visor upside down and slightly crooked. When I saw him maneuvering his way through the crowded hallway toward me, I never expected him to stop and talk to me, but that is exactly what he did.

"Hey," he said, his blue eyes focusing on me.

"Hi," I answered, narrowing my eyes.

"Where are you from?" he asked.

"Here," I said as I crossed my arms over my chest. His name was Jake Olsen. A few of the "troublemakers" knew him already, but he was the new kid to most of us.

"You mean you've lived here your whole life?"

"Yes," I said putting on my best annoyed face.

"Wow," he said. "Do you know James Williams?"

"Who?"

"James Williams," he repeated.

"No."

"Oh." He was silent during a moment of thought. "Do you know Derek Bryan?"

"No," I said, starting to get suspicious. Why the heck was this guy talking to me? And who were these random people he was asking me about?

"You don't?" he asked in utter surprise.

"No," I said for a third time as the furrow between my eyebrows got deeper. Jake had moved to my high school from Stoneville High, the school in the city right next to the town in which I lived. When you go to a small high school, it is easy to learn information about all the other students there. Secrets are hardly ever kept. So I already knew what I needed to know about Jake. He had built himself a colorful reputation.

"Well, you have to know Keith White," he said with confidence.

"Actually, I don't," I said as I recrossed my arms. Jake fell silent, but the look of surprise returned to his face. It was as if I was in the middle of a battle. I was determined to hold my ground. But at first I wasn't sure why I was fighting and why he felt like my adversary. So, as I stared Jake Olsen down, I weighed the possibilities in my mind. I assumed that these people were from Stoneville High. But why would he assume that I knew them? Did he think I was someone else? Then it hit me. My annoyance started to turn into anger. These people were black. I was past ready for this boy to leave my personal space.

"Really? You don't know Keith?"

"I don't." I glared. He stepped back as if my look had injured him. Awkwardly, he said good-bye and continued on his way. I figured I had won the battle, sort of. But it didn't exactly feel good. I couldn't have been angrier as I turned away from his disappearing figure and walked toward my next class. I spent the rest of the day irritated with him and anyone else who dared to look at me funny. Not long after my "discussion" with Jake, I learned that he had transferred to yet another high school. Therefore Jake and I never had another chance to cross paths in the halls, and, in all honesty, I was perfectly satisfied with never having to see him again.

I saved my own life. It was simple—not easy, but simple. I just changed the way I thought about myself and other people. When I say I saved my life, I do not mean that I saved myself from physical death. I saved myself from emotional and mental death. I was close to becoming one of those dangerous cynics devoid of any empathy and sympathy, a woman who lacked any real hope for the improvement of humanity. If I never developed those characteristics, I would consider myself dead in some sense. Since I now live to uphold these qualities, my life without them would be empty.

My experience in high school created the path toward the mental and emotional death that I ultimately avoided. While in high school, I had the desire to fit in. Of course, the struggle to fit in is difficult for all teenagers. However, being a black girl in a predominantly white high school complicated this issue for me. Many people would have labeled my difficulty a "black pride" thing. They would say that if my parents had taught me to be proud of my heritage, I would not have had the problem I did. These people would be mistaken. My heritage was not the problem. The issue was not pride or shame. The problem was that some people saw me as black first and as Nicole, the individual, second. What seemed to matter the most about me to quite a few people was my blackness—the thing that separated me from other people. I was an "other," and people treated me as such. Sure, from time to time, others called me disparaging names and excluded me from things because of my race. (I was lucky that I did not experience too much of that sort of thing.) However, (and probably more importantly), I was not given the dignity of individualism that most of my white classmates and friends enjoyed.

Many of my teachers and peers assumed that my interests lay in African American history or jazz and hip-hop (basically anything to do with black people), never taking into account that one of my favorite writers was Oscar Wilde or that I enjoyed Broadway musicals and Shakespeare. I was black first, lumped into a group, stripped of any possible uniqueness. Those who made these assumptions implied that I was less than they were by attempting to deny me my individuality. They refused to recognize the possibility that I had an existence other than that of their preconceived notion of a "black person." For four years, I fought against those assumptions. I tried repeatedly to prove that I was more than a "black person." I fought as if my life depended on it (and at the time I felt it did), but I never proved that I was a full and complete person. I failed miserably, and I was devastated.

I failed because I was fighting a losing battle. I lost it the minute I started fighting. Going into the fight meant that I thought I had something to gain or lose. However, I was fighting a battle that would give me nothing even if I won. I was born an individual and a full human being just like everyone else. Nothing could take that away from me. Nevertheless, I was putting my innate personhood on the table for questioning as if it were something to debate. My desire to prove my individuality was not meant to influence those in my community; it was meant to influence me. In short, I doubted myself, and in my attempt to prove to others that I was worthy of personhood, I was trying to convince myself of my worthiness.

Of course, at the time, I had no idea that this was the case. All I knew was that I was angry with everyone who I felt denied me my full individuality, and they were wrong to do so. I blamed them for my horrible high-school experience, and I do not think anyone would fault me for that. High school would have been different if some of my teachers and peers had not been racist (if the world had not been racist). But racism was—and still is—very real in this society. I could not change that. I could fight racism tooth and nail (and I did and still do) but I could not guarantee how my efforts would manifest themselves. Besides, I was suffering at that particular point in time, and I could not rely on the unlikely event of racism ending in my lifetime as a means to supply me with peace of mind. I needed immediate help because I was losing faith in the world at that moment.

I distrusted almost everyone. I made few friends because fewer people in my life meant fewer battles. I was lonely. I was sad. I hated my life. And worse yet, even after I left high school, the place I had deemed my living hell, those feelings still continued.

I had always been close to my father and felt that I could talk to him about anything. Since we were close, it was easy for my father to see how sad I was, so he offered something to help me through it. He spoon-fed me *Withstanding the Lie*. I was skeptical about the effectiveness of what he was telling me, but I tried it. I had nothing to lose.

My father started by reminding me of my innate personhood by telling me that I was worth something just because I was alive. He told me—and it took me a while to realize what he was saying—that I was worthy of anything and everything on this earth just like every other person who was breathing this air. No one can claim to be better than anyone else. You may be older, you may have more money, and you may be more popular, but you are not any better than I am. We all abide by the same rules of the universe: We all need food and oxygen to live, and we all eventually die. This may be bad news for those who are high on the social totem pole, for those who have been feeling good about themselves because society deems them better than the rest of the world. But for those who feel as if they have been sloshing in the mud of society, this is great news. You and I, we are worth something.

Once I came to this realization, I stopped fighting battles that I could not win. I did not carry the burden of proof. Once I understood why I was trying to prove my worthiness to others, I was able to concentrate on loving myself. I took the outside world out of the equation when it came to understanding my worthiness. When others told me that I was unworthy, I knew they were wrong, and I knew they were lying. I do not fight the lie. I fight the liar, but not the lie. I have better things to do with my time and energy.

The liar is like some idiot in your face telling you that you have seven eyes when you know you only have two. In these situations, you can try to justify yourself or see the lie for what it is. The mature thing to do is to see the lie for what it is. However, before I adopted this new attitude, I felt a need to prove my individuality. But every time I fought the lie, I was emotionally and mentally beaten. It punched and kicked me, because I had opened myself up to it. Time and time again, I walked right into the liar's trap—thinking that each time I fought the battle to prove that I was worthy, I had a chance to win. I now understand that my efforts were futile.

Once I began to accept that worthiness as a human being is internal and innate, not only was I able to stop fighting losing battles in my everyday life, but I was also able to begin to let go of all the anger I felt surrounding my high-school experience. Of course, this was all easier said than done. I had to adopt a new *lifestyle*. A new way of thinking had to permeate my entire life. As such, it took commitment and practice. It took constant reminders and setbacks. It took patience and persistence. And I had to acknowledge that I was beginning something that would never end. I would never master the techniques needed for rethinking my life. Sure, I would get better at them (and hopefully very good at them), but there would always be difficult days, complicated situations, and times of regression.

Therefore the techniques of *Withstanding the Lie* saved my life. God only knows where I would be if I had not made this lifestyle change. I probably would have been sitting in a rocking chair on my front porch, years later, mumbling to my grandchildren about how folks are always out to "getcha." I would still be miserable and angry. And I would definitely be lonely. No matter how much you love her, who really looks forward to visiting a crotchety grandmother?

I am sure my negative feelings would have eventually consumed me. I would have set out for a life of underachievement, doing only what society claimed I could do. Thus I would not have pursued the opportunities that I did. I would not have spent three years studying creative writing and discovering my passion for it. I would not have traveled to foreign countries. I would not have continued to study music. I would not have even dreamed of moving to New York City and attending graduate school. And I certainly would not have coauthored a book. All this happened because I was able to withstand the lie and recognize my innate worthiness as a human being. I only know this now by looking back. I began using the techniques because I was tired of being hopeless and wounded. I wanted to feel better. Little did I know that I was actually changing the direction of my life and writing myself a new future.

It is important to note that *Withstanding the Lie* is not a recipe for a magnificent existence. It is not a promise of getting everything you desire. So many things that I have wanted have passed me by. In fact, I have had more unfulfilled desires since I changed my lifestyle. I am taking more chances, which means I am experiencing more failures. Instead,

Withstanding the Lie is a collection of techniques for protecting yourself from the attitudes that are meant to harm you and prevent you from striving for the life that you desire. People will stand in your way. Racist, sexist, and homophobic people will stand in your way. They always do, and sometimes you just cannot get around them. But your inner self does not have to be severely damaged from these situations. You can face them, move through them, and remain standing tall. It is a possible and glorious thing. I know because I have tried it and have had success.

Adopting these techniques reminds me of the time I first started wearing glasses in the sixth grade. I remember putting them on, stepping outside and looking at the street with amazement. The world looked so much sharper and clearer. I was seeing everything as it truly was, but the world had not changed. I had changed with the aid of my brand-new glasses. And, as it always is with new glasses, once you have been wearing them for a while, you find yourself wondering how you ever got around without them.

So, like a nearsighted sixth grader who can finally see the chalkboard without squinting, I invite you to live your life seeing the world devoid of the limitations of self-deprecation. You will never know what you have been missing until you put on your new way of thinking, living, and being, and stare out into the world.

INTRODUCTION
By Roger

I AM ONE of twelve children born to my mother and father. At the time of my birth, my parents were sharecroppers. A landowner provided a place for us to live and made a profit from our labor on the farm. My older brothers and sisters and I worked with our parents in the fields. Cotton and corn were our primary crops. Abject poverty was our economic status. We lived in shacks infested with rats and bedbugs. We wore ragged shoes and clothes. We ate pork and chicken as provided by the animals we raised on the farm. We ate peas, beans, corn, and other vegetables from our gardens. At times, however, we only had milk and cornbread, sugar biscuits, and boiled rice.

In those days, as sharecroppers we were required by law to attend racially segregated schools that were far inferior to the schools provided for whites. In addition, my older brothers and sisters and I were kept out of school for a period of two to three months each school year to work on the farm. We broke the grounds and cultivated the crops with mules hooked to plows. We hoed grass and weeds from the fields. We picked cotton, gathered corn, milked cows, harvested hay, and did other hard labor as required.

As black people, we were denied access to restaurants, hotels, theaters, and other public accommodations, except as provided, if at all, in a separate and degrading manner. Racial segregation, employment discrimination, discrimination in housing, and other racist practices were dictated by culture and also required by law.

My great fortune in life is that I received a precious gift from my mother when I was a young boy. It served to protect me from loss of self-esteem and other mental and emotional injuries as I was growing up in poverty and racial oppression and also in the years that followed, continuing even to this day. My mother's gift was that she taught my brothers and sisters and me that we were inferior to no one. She said some people might have more talent. She said some people might have more money, better homes, and more material possessions. She said some people might not treat you the way you should be treated. But no matter what, she told each of us, you are a precious human being, and nobody anywhere in the world is more precious than you.

I realize today that what my mother taught my brothers and sisters and me about our value as human beings is very different from other thoughts and messages about self-worth conveyed to us by society. Many people believe that a person's value as a human being is dependent on his or her achievement, physical appearance, talent, social status, or other aspects of an outward or material nature. But that is not what my mother believed. My mother taught us that our value as human beings is now and everlasting and does not depend on anybody or anything in the material world.

As you might expect, the poverty and state-compelled racial oppression in which I found myself as a young person did not totally occupy my life. I had other very important things of a more positive nature also going on. I was nourished by the love and support of family, friends, teachers, preachers, and others. I had many fun and uplifting activities in my life such as games, celebrations, achievements, and family gatherings that brought me much joy and pleasure despite the poverty and racism I have described. No question about it, the love, support, and joy I experienced in my youth contributed much to my sense of self-worth. Nevertheless, my mother's teachings provided a huge advantage to me in protecting myself from mental and emotional harm otherwise caused by the bigotry, prejudice, and poverty I encountered. She said we were valuable human beings, just as valuable as anyone or everyone else in the world, and nobody—nothing—could take that away from us. I heard what she said, and I believed her.

I did not like the poverty and racial oppression into which I was born. I was hurt and disappointed by the way I was treated. I wanted to improve not only my own life, but also the lives of family members and others who experienced racism and poverty as I did. But I was not overwhelmed by the circumstances of the day. I was not diminished on the inside. I was always up on my toes, always leaning forward, always filled with hope and focused on getting the very best out of the life I had to live.

I enlisted in the military when I turned eighteen. My exposure to different people, places, ideas, and experiences opened up the wider world to me. I could see and understand more fully the opportunities available to me, and I could see how to take advantage of those opportunities. After I left the military, I pursued higher education, graduated from college, completed law school, and entered the practice of law. I achieved outstanding results as a trial attorney for a national insurance company and was promoted in the course of my employment to regional managing attorney. After twenty-nine years in the profession, I retired from the practice of law to spend more time sharing what I know about protecting oneself from the loss of self-esteem and other mental and emotional harm caused by bigotry and prejudice.

Significant achievement in life for many in our society involves a fair share of denials, disappointments, setbacks, failures, and other adversity along the way. Achievement for me was certainly no different. Undeniably, not all of the adversity I experienced was related to race, but race still played a huge role. After the abolition of state-compelled racial oppression in the United States, most of the bigotry I encountered was subtle in nature; while people might not directly deny me a material benefit, they would nevertheless state or imply that I was inferior as a human being. Naturally I was hurt and discouraged when things did not evolve or turn out as I had hoped. But through all of it, I never felt inferior to anyone as a human being. I never felt defeated or diminished at the core of who and what I am.

Considering the poverty and racism into which I was born, I would not have achieved things in life at the level I have described, nor would I have experienced or continue to experience the quality of life that I know today, had I not believed in my value as a human being as taught to me by my mother. My unconditional sense of self-worth empowered me to pursue my dreams and aspirations and enabled me to persevere. I persevered despite the challenges I faced and the odds against my success. My sense of self-worth also provided me with a continuous overall sense of inner peace and self-satisfaction.

Now I am certainly not claiming or suggesting, even for a moment, that I have accomplished everything in my life that I want or wanted to accomplish. Absolutely not! Many things I have wanted in my life never happened. I continue today to have frustrations and disappointments. I continue today to encounter bigotry and prejudice. But at the same time I am proud of my accomplishments, and I am very pleased with my life. I do not harbor hostility or anger, and I feel complete on the inside. The quality of life that I have lived and continue to live is due directly to how I feel about myself as a human being.

The same belief that my mother taught my brothers and sisters and me about our value as human beings is a huge component of the strategy to protect yourself that Nicole and I are recommending in this book. Perhaps you already know and practice this powerful belief in your life. If so, how great it is. Whatever the case may be, if you suffer bigotry and prejudice, Nicole and I believe what we have to offer in this book will greatly improve the quality of your life.

Total dignity and respect in our society is still a long way off. But you do not have to wait for some uncertain date in the future, when all bigotry is resolved, to fully live the life that has been given to you. The bigotry and prejudice you suffer need not make you feel your life is incomplete.

You do not have to live your life envying others who appear to have all of the advantages. The people you envy do not necessarily have better quality in their lives than you. Continue to stand up for your rights and privileges. Continue to work hard for a fair and just society. At the same time, take up your life right now and live it completely, not with hostility, not with despair, not with self-pity, not with regret or submission, but as a special gift to you in your time here on the planet. The principles and practices articulated in *Withstanding the Lie* can help you do so in a powerful and significant way.

PART 1

The young boy whose lunch is snatched by a bully on the playground cries more from intimidation and humiliation than from the loss of his peanut-butter-and-jelly sandwich.

MACK

THERE IS A story about a dog named Mack. One day this dog named Mack just showed up at the front door of Billy T. Hudson's house.

Billy T. Hudson and his wife named Carrie Ann had eight children, and they all lived on Hill Creek Road, about halfway down the hill on the right-hand side before you get to the creek.

When the dog named Mack showed up at the house, the children went out to look at him. They could see right away that he had just one eye. It was his right eye. His left eye looked like somebody had poked it out. It was all closed up and everything with some healed-up skin all around it. Mack also had a healed-up scar down the middle of his nose where it looked like somebody had hit him with something.

The children kept on looking at Mack. Then they saw he had a crooked right hind leg what made him hop when he walked. His right hind foot didn't touch the ground like his other feet. It looked like that right hind leg got broke, and, when it healed up, it just healed up crooked and everything.

There was a spot on Mack's left hindquarter where no hair was growing. The skin what you saw was all healed up, but it wasn't smooth like you might think. It was kinda rough-looking. Billy T. said later that he bet somebody shot at the dog with a shotgun and missed most of him, but just hit him on the side like that.

There were some more scars on Mack's sides and under his belly, too, but they were so little the children didn't pay too much attention to them.

After everybody had looked Mack over real good and everything, the boy named Sammy said, "Let's run that dog off somewhere." But the girl named Sarah Mae took a liking to the dog and said no. She sat down next to him and gave him the name Mack.

The boy named Chesterfield brought the other dogs into the yard from out in the fields where he'd been playing with them. The other dogs ran around in the yard just barking and swishing their tails and playing with everybody and everything. But Mack just sat there. Sarah Mae told Mack, "Mack, you get up and play." But Mack didn't do anything. He just kept sitting there looking at everybody.

When Billy T. came home that evening from working in the fields, and everybody was sitting around eating supper, Sarah Mae took her plate and sat next to her daddy.

"Did you see the dog, Daddy?"

Billy T. nodded.

"What's the matter with him?" Sarah Mae asked.

"Whatcha mean, 'what's the matter with him?'" Billy T. asked.

"He don't bark like the other dogs. He won't say nothing."

"Look like he's been beat up."

"Ain't nothing wrong with his mouth, but he still won't bark," Sarah Mae said.

"How do you know ain't nothing wrong with his mouth?"

"'Cause I looked in it."

"That dog won't run around and play like the other dogs," Chesterfield chimed in.

"Well, he's crippled, ain't he?" Billy T. said.

"Yeah, but he could run around on his other three legs, if he wanted to."

"That dog walk around with his head down," the girl named Ella Jean added. "Why he walk around all the time with his head down?"

"What's the matter with the dog, Daddy?" Sarah Mae persisted.

Billy T. couldn't figure out what to tell 'em in the way they wanted to know.

That Sunday, two of Billy T.'s brothers came over to the house for a visit. They were sitting around with Billy T. on the front porch, talking about this and that. Mack was on the porch, too, just lying around looking at everybody. It seemed like that dog knowed everything what everybody was saying. But everybody knows a dog can't understand people-talk, except a few words. But the way Mack was sitting there listening and everything made Billy T. a little uneasy.

"Get away from here, you old dog! Go out there somewhere, and do something!" Billy T. shouted. But Mack just sat there. Then Billy T. grabbed a stick to run the dog off. Sarah Mae was standing in the yard and saw what was happening. She came up and nudged Mack and got him to move off the porch.

In the next few days, the children kept on trying to get Mack to bark. They got up in his face and started barking like dogs themselves. They thought if Mack saw them barking, he might start barking, too. But Mack wouldn't do nothing, except he would just look and listen. The children also tried to get Mack to run and play. They pushed him, jumped over him, made all kinda noise and everything, and did whatever else they could think of. One time they even brought the cat out and put the cat up in his face to try to make him mad. He just looked at the cat and didn't do nothing.

Billy T. saw some of what the children were doing with the dog but didn't know quite what to make of it. And it worried Billy T. to have that crippled dog around the house at all, especially since he was acting like he knowed what folks were saying, like he had as much sense as a person. So Billy T. got up early one morning and grabbed the dog and put him in the back of his pickup truck. He drove somewhere about ten miles to a place on a dirt road where there were no houses, just woods and swamp on both sides. He took the dog off the truck and left him there. When he drove off, he looked in his rearview mirror. Mack didn't try to follow. He just sat there on the side of the road with his head down.

Sarah Mae missed the dog very much and the other children did, too. They kept asking one another if anybody had seen Mack. Billy T. didn't have the nerve to tell anybody what he had done. Then, a few days later, the dog showed up again at the front door. The children were happy to see him, and they went back to trying to get him to bark and play and everything, but he never would.

Billy T. decided that since the children liked the dog so much, it wouldn't be right to sneak around and haul him off again. But he was still troubled because in his mind Mack was a peculiar dog. He figured that if that dog was going be around for a while, he'd better try to get to the bottom of everything and understand what the dog was all about. So, the first chance he got, he sat down in front of the dog and started staring at him right in his face. But Mack wouldn't look back at Billy T. With his one eye open, he looked down and away. Then Billy T. took Mack by the head and tried to make Mack look back at him. He moved Mack's head anyway he wanted, but Mack still wouldn't look him in the eye.

When Billy T. saw that Mack wouldn't look him in the eye, he started thinking about everything. He started thinking that Mack had been mistreated for so long that he didn't feel he was worth anything. He figured Mack felt stupid all the time and that's why he couldn't do anything right and most of the times wouldn't even try. Billy T. knowed that in everything Mack had been through, his heart had been broken in an awful kinda way and he was feeling like he was no more than nothing on the inside.

Billy T. got kinda sad and almost started to cry, but he was able to hold everything back. He looked around to make sure none of the children was looking at him. He was so bothered by what he knowed about the dog that he didn't know exactly what he ought to do next. So he went and got a fresh pail of water for the dog to drink and put it in front of him. And then he went inside and brought back a biscuit, and he watched the dog drink the water and eat the biscuit.

The next day, when everybody woke up in the morning, the dog was gone again. The whole Hudson family, Billy T. and all, was upset about that. For two or three days in a row, Billy T. drove Sarah Mae around looking for the dog, but he was nowhere to be found. Everybody kept thinking that maybe one day Mack would come back, but he never did, and after a while everybody just gave up hope. The dog named Mack was never seen again, not even till this day.

Truth Be Told
(Early Encounters with Bigotry)

Nicole

IT WAS MILK time—time to decide what kind of milk you wanted for lunch: regular, skim, or chocolate. It was a daily occurrence for a kindergartener, like tying your shoes or brushing your teeth—just something you had to do.

The milk procedure was simple. We each had a small orange disk (a circular piece of cardboard covered with orange construction paper) to place in one of the milk containers so that Mrs. Robinson and her milk-helper for the day could count the number of skim, regular, and chocolate milks for that day's lunch. When Mrs. Robinson called us, we would drop our disks in one of the three containers on her desk. The containers were old milk cartons with their tops cut off—a green carton for skim milk, a red carton for regular milk, and a brown carton for chocolate milk. I knew what I was getting. I was going to put my orange disk in the red carton on the end. Regular milk, just like always. Stick to the routine.

"You should get chocolate milk," the boy next to me said. I stared at him.

"Chocolate milk?"

He looked at me and nodded. The teacher called the table in front of us. I clutched my disk.

I never thought about having chocolate milk. I had always had regular milk at home. Wait. Was I supposed to have chocolate milk? Was there some rule about it that no one had ever told me about?

The teacher called our table. I was last in line. I stared at the three boxes. My orange disk thudded on the bottom of the brown chocolate milk box. I looked up at Mrs. Robinson, and she smiled.

ROGER

I realized, to my surprise actually, that I was in a restaurant. I don't recall the specific details of how a young boy like me ended up walking in there alone. I was seven to ten years old. However, I remember clearly that people were seated at the various tables eating their meals. Sharp eyes turned and focused on me, and immediately I knew something was wrong, but I didn't precisely understand the problem. I was frightened and didn't know quite what to do. My first thought was to get out of there. But I didn't want to do anything that could be interpreted as hostile. It was clear in my mind that my offending conduct, whatever it was, was more than sufficient. My concern was that if I walked out abruptly, I would make things worse, and I didn't want to do anything to exacerbate the situation. As I stood there, my hope was that someone would give me a sign, no words necessary, just a clear sign of what I should do, and I would promptly abide.

The eyes were still focused on me, and my heart was pounding. Without any further deliberation, I took a chance and turned and walked out of the door. I moved swiftly up the sidewalk. Suddenly, I heard a screaming voice behind me.

"Hey! Hey!"

I stopped and looked in that direction. There was a man standing on the sidewalk in front of the restaurant.

"I told ya'll before," he shouted at the top of his voice. "Don't ever come inside. Go around to the back window if you want something, and I'll bring it out there to you!"

The harsh and bitter tone of the man's voice was unmistakable in its meaning. I did not belong in that restaurant. I continued up the sidewalk, without responding, feeling degraded and more uncertain than before about the world situation.

It was not until later that I truly appreciated what had happened. Black people were not permitted to enter public restaurants, except for a few owned by blacks. Of course, I understood segregation. My confusion was that I had been permitted to enter downtown stores to buy things, provided I was totally deferential to whites in my behavior. I thought I could do likewise and enter the restaurant—a huge mistake on my part.

NICOLE

She was the new girl, and it was exciting. Amanda and I couldn't wait for recess. Who wouldn't want a new friend? She was sitting on a giant tire eating M&M'S. Amanda and I went to join her along with Rachel and Jessica. She was passing out handfuls of M&M'S. We stood at the tire smiling at her—one handful for Jessica, one handful for Rachel, one handful for Amanda.

She stopped and looked up at me. Her piercing blue eyes focused on my face.

"I don't share with black people," she said in a low voice. Everything seemed to stop. All eyes were on me. I looked at my feet and then backed away.

"Come on; let's go," Amanda said. She gave her M&M'S back to the girl, and we walked away together, leaving Rachel, Jessica, and the new girl behind. I watched the ground as we walked away. I didn't look at Amanda, knowing that if I took the risk of making eye contact, I might not be able to suppress the tears welling up in my eyes.

We stopped at the swing set, and I sat on the swing. I tucked my feet in and out, harder and faster until I could hear nothing but the wind whipping past my ears—nothing but the howling air.

ROGER

My feet rustled the fallen leaves as I ran zigzagging between the trees, dodging imaginary dangers. I then sprinted into an open area as fast as

I could, imagining that the wind would engulf me and lift my body high into the air above the tree branches and treetops. But I did not get a lift, not even in my imagination.

I was nothing but alone in the woods. I would go there to play, and in my imagination I could be anyone I wanted to be. I could travel to any place of my desire, on earth and beyond. But on this occasion, my magical powers had been taken away, and I could not fly.

My mother had been driving home alone earlier that day when two white men in another car forced her off the road. They made threatening gestures at her and called her disparaging names before speeding away, their tires squealing on the blacktop.

As a young boy, the woods in rural Georgia were my sanctuary. They were my freedom and my magic. But on that particular day, the magic was not there.

Soon I was able to fly again and again and visit faraway places. But in the days and weeks immediately following the attack on my mother, my flying was not as light and easy as before, and the faraway places were not as lucid or inviting.

THE TALK OF TERRYTON

STATE SENATOR ELEANOR Culpepper is a sixty-one-year-old, healthy woman of average height and size. There is nothing outstanding, one way or the other, in her physical appearance. One might describe her as an ordinary-looking woman. But there is nothing ordinary about her in her strength and character. She is a very capable leader who is highly respected by others, especially by the people she represents in her senatorial district. Each of the different groups in her district, the whites, the blacks, the liberals, the conservatives, or what have you, believes she likes their group the best. But make no mistake about it: Eleanor Culpepper does not compromise her integrity to make people happy. She speaks her mind and does what she feels is right. She does so and still treats everyone with dignity and respect because she believes in her heart everyone should be treated that way.

Eleanor follows the example of her father. Her father, the highly respected Ernest Till who died at the age of eighty-seven, served the public well during his lifetime, first as a state representative and afterward as senator for the Sixteenth District for a total period spanning two decades. A huge part of his legacy was his leadership in integrating public schools and other public accommodations in Terry County during the 1960s and continuing into the 1970s. Some counties in the state struggled with integration at that time, but not Terry County, due primarily to the leadership of Mr. Till. He was bold in telling his constituents that integration was going to happen and that it was the right thing to do. Some people didn't like what he was saying, but he moved them forward nevertheless with his powerful credibility and integrity of character.

Terryton has a population of about twenty thousand people. It is the county seat for Terry County and is included in the Sixteenth Senatorial District. Eleanor lives in Terryton and has an office in the town as well. She first learned that some in the Terryton community were engaged in potentially harmful chatter and speculation when she and her husband Zack attended the county fair. The county fair was held annually on the fairgrounds just north of Terryton, beginning on the third Friday of each September and continuing three days through Sunday.

Eleanor and Zack arrived at the fair early Saturday afternoon, as was their usual practice. They walked around together on the fairgrounds engaging friends, constituents, acquaintances, and even strangers with greetings and brief conversation. Interacting with people in this way was without question a benefit to Eleanor in her political career, but she and her husband also genuinely enjoyed the experience.

The fair had different food booths that sold sandwiches, fries, ice cream, and pastries. Also, there were arts-and-crafts displays, baking contests, different farm animals in temporary stables, tractors and other outdoor equipment on display, amusement rides, an outdoor stage for bands and other performances, and two rest areas with portable tables and chairs for people to sit and eat or just relax.

Eleanor and Zack stopped to relax in the rest area near the east entrance. They were seated at a table, each with a beverage, when Eleanor noticed Don Newell, the principal of Terryton High School, walking in their direction.

Don had called Eleanor's office the day before. Eleanor was in a meeting at the time and could not take his call. Don left a message requesting a return call. When Eleanor returned his call, he was not available. She left him a message but did not follow up further.

"I called you back and left a message," Eleanor said to Don.

"I know," Don replied. "Thought it was a good chance I'd see you here today."

"You two need to talk business?" Zack asked.

"I wouldn't call it business," Don answered.

"You know what?" Zack stated, rising from his seat. "I think I'll take a walk."

"You don't have to do that on my part," Don stated.

"I'll take a walk," Zack responded and walked away in the direction of the arts-and-crafts displays. Zack supported his wife completely, but he was careful to give her space to attend to her political affairs.

Don sat down in a chair at the table across from Eleanor. Eleanor knew Don in the same way she knew other leaders in Terryton. She also knew him as a relative, the oldest child of her first cousin, Amy.

"What's going on, Don?" Eleanor asked. "Something wrong?"

"'Wrong' might not be the right word."

"OK, but you're obviously concerned about something. Talk to me."

"Well, when you say 'what's going on,'" Don admitted, "something *is* going on. Something is going on with the black people, you know, the African Americans." He hesitated for a moment, trying to read Eleanor's initial reaction.

Eleanor preferred that he get right to the point, "Something's going on; I hear that. You gonna tell me what you're talking about?"

"A few of the teachers picked it up from the black students in their classrooms. We don't know exactly what they're doing, but as best we can tell, they've got something going on in their minds."

"You think?" Eleanor asked sarcastically.

"No, I mean it. You can tell *something* is going on. Sometimes you can hear them saying things out loud."

"What kind of things are they saying, Don?" Eleanor asked, growing a bit impatient.

"Things like, 'up a tree' and 'there ain't no bogeyman.'"

"'Up a tree' and 'there ain't no bogeyman'?" Eleanor chuckled out loud.

"I'm not kidding, Eleanor."

"Up a tree, there ain't no bogeyman? That makes absolutely no sense to me."

"It appears they're trying to accomplish something. We've noticed," Don explained, "that they don't seem to be concerned that they're black."

"What an odd thing to say. Sounds like crap to me," Eleanor chastised.

"I'm not a bigot, Eleanor. You know me. I wouldn't go there. What I'm saying is that they still stand up for themselves and they still want to make things better, as far as we can tell. But they just don't seem to be bothered that they're living in a society that has prejudice against them."

Don noticed that a middle-aged black woman and two young children were taking seats at the next table over. In such close proximity, Don felt he had to be guarded in the words he used in his conversation with Eleanor. A white man and a white woman sitting next to a black woman talking about black people made him a bit uncomfortable.

"How do you know that?" Eleanor asked Don.

"How do I know what?"

"How do you *know* the black students have this kind of peace of mind that you're talking about?"

"The teachers see it."

"Yes, but what are they seeing, Don? What are the teachers seeing that makes them say there is a change in the black students?"

"Well, there is no dramatic improvement in their grades, if that's what you're asking. Not yet, anyway, but we're keeping an eye on that."

Eleanor looked away momentarily, and Don was irritated by her response. He wouldn't say it out loud, but he wanted to remind Eleanor that he is a highly respected high-school principal, not that little boy his mom used to bring to family gatherings.

"Maybe you're right, Eleanor. Perhaps we *are* just making it up," Don asserted.

"Nobody said you're making it up."

"The only thing I can say," Don stated firmly, "is that the teachers know their students and they see a change in how the black students interact with the teachers and other students. You can't see inside

15

somebody's mind, I grant you that, but you can see attitude and demeanor. The black students are not timid or anxious like I used to see with some of them. The best way to describe it is that they act like they belong, you know what I mean? There's no swagger or anything like that, but I have to tell you, they act like they belong. And you can't single out one thing in particular to prove it. It's just a lot of little things adding up."

"OK," Eleanor conceded, "I hear what you're saying."

Don continued, "This is not coming from just one teacher. I have three teachers in particular who are adamant about it. They first started seeing something back in April or May before the summer break. And now with everyone back for the new school year, they're seeing the same thing."

Don and Eleanor could overhear the conversation at the next table. The two young children were asking the middle-aged woman, their "grandma," to take them directly to the amusement rides. "Not yet," Grandma insisted. She was giving the youngsters a brief time out. They were not being nice to each other because of a dispute over whose turn it was to sit in the front seat of the car during their drive to the fair.

"Look, I understand your skepticism," Don persisted with Eleanor. "I wasn't persuaded so quickly myself. That's why I'm just now saying something about it."

"I'm not trying to give you a hard time," Eleanor answered, "I just want to understand what you're telling me."

Don did not have an immediate response to Eleanor's words, and a moment of silence fell upon them. Eleanor broke the silence, "At peace with themselves, even though there is prejudice against them," she summarized.

"Yes," Don said, nodding, "but some of them are more at peace than others. Like I said, I think it's something they're working on. And if the high-school students are working on it, you can bet your breeches that it's going on in the whole black community as well."

Don realized, immediately after he had done so, that he had used the term "black community." He glanced over quickly to see if the woman at the next table had noticed. It did not appear to him that she had.

"You know what, Don," Eleanor calmly stated, "it's not a bad thing when people are at peace with themselves."

"But the natural reaction, when society has prejudice against you, is to be upset about it," Don argued.

"An educator like you—have you forgotten the nursery rhyme, 'sticks and stones may break my bones, but words will never hurt me'?"

"But a nursery rhyme is precisely that, a nursery rhyme. It's not the real world."

"Perhaps it can be."

"I hear what you're saying, but the reality today is that words do hurt."

Eleanor noticed in her peripheral vision someone waving to her from the walk path nearby. She looked directly and recognized a senior gentleman standing there as others walked past him. She had met the man at a fundraising event but could not recall his name at the moment. He had recently moved to town from out of state.

"Hello, Senator," the man called out to Eleanor.

"Hello to you as well," Eleanor shouted back, "I hope you're enjoying the fair."

"You betcha."

"Did you see the tractors and lawn equipment?"

"As a matter of fact, I'm headed that way."

With those words said, Eleanor waved to the man. The man waved again and was on his way.

Eleanor turned her attention back to Don. "Don, are you threatened by the way these students are behaving? I want to understand your concern."

"I wouldn't say threatened," Don answered. "At this point, I don't know what we're dealing with in the first place."

"Would you consider talking to the students?" Eleanor challenged. "Why don't you ask the students themselves? And what about the black teachers? You have black teachers on the staff. Why don't you ask them?"

Mindful of the black people at the next table, Don was a little uneasy that Eleanor was boldly using the words "black teachers" and "black students."

"I can't go around asking the teachers and students, Eleanor. You know that."

"Who says you can't?" Eleanor pushed back. "If something is going on, and you want to know what it is, who says you can't ask?"

"I don't feel comfortable doing that. You know, they might be offended or something."

"Don, these black people you're talking about—you're not scared of them, are you? My goodness, they are your students. The teachers are people you work with. These are your brothers and sisters, Don, your fellow citizens; you do understand that, don't you?"

"My point," Don answered, "is that nobody has broken any laws or regulations, that I can see, or even engaged in any inappropriate behavior whatsoever. Some may consider it offensive or even intimidating if I were to suddenly start asking questions."

Eleanor took a moment to consider Don's reasoning and acknowledged to herself that he had a point.

"Eleanor, I came to you for advice," Don continued. "That's what I'm looking for—a bit of guidance, that's all. At this point, I didn't go to the superintendent, the mayor, or anyone else up the chain of command, so to speak. Sort of keeping it quiet. At this point, I'm just looking for a little advice from family."

"But if the teachers know," Eleanor responded, "then the friends and relatives of the teachers also know, and the friends and relatives of the friends and relatives probably know as well. Who knows? By now we may have all kinds of speculation, and who knows what else, running around all over the place."

"Time out" was over. The woman and two youngsters at the next table stood up and started walking in the direction of the amusement rides.

At the same time, Eleanor rose from her seat. "I'm going to catch up with Zack," she said. "Actually we have a few errands to run."

"I understand," Don responded.

"Do me a favor," Eleanor continued. "Don't overreact to this thing. That's my family advice. Don't overreact. And give me a couple of days. I need to have a talk with a friend."

Eleanor then walked away in the direction that Zack had walked earlier.

Don had not expected any one thing in particular from Eleanor. But he certainly expected more than what she had offered. He was disappointed with their conversation.

Michael, a sixty-one-year-old black man, is generally regarded as handsome in physical appearance. He owns an insurance agency and employs two support workers who assist him in selling motor-vehicle and homeowner insurance to the public. Michael is also a leader in his church and the wider local community. Previously, he served four years as a member of the Terry County Board of Education. He works "behind the scenes" along with other leaders identifying and developing promising individuals who would be good candidates for elected or appointed public office.

At twelve thirty precisely, Michael entered The Palace, the most prestigious restaurant in Terryton, wearing a dress shirt, dress shoes, and pleated trousers. The hostess greeted him immediately and said, "Mr. Hobson, I will escort you to your table."

The restaurant was in no way filled with diners at the time, but there were a good number of people seated at various tables having lunch. Michael followed the hostess across the main dining room floor to a more private dining area near the rear.

Eleanor was seated there alone at a table. She rose from her seat as Michael approached.

"Hello, Michael," she said, extending her hand.

"Hello, Senator," Michael responded, shaking her hand.

"First thing, drop the formality, will you. I'm having lunch with a friend."

"In that case, hello, Eleanor."

"Please sit."

Eleanor noticed that Michael was carrying a briefcase, which he placed on the floor next to himself as both he and Eleanor sat down at the table.

"Your server will be here shortly," the hostess stated and then moved back across the floor in the direction of her station at the front entrance.

"Michael, do you know why I invited you to lunch?" Eleanor asked.

"I think so," Michael answered, "you did mention something about what's going on in the community."

"I want to be up-front with you."

"As far as I can tell, you're always up-front with me."

Eleanor and Michael had known each other since they were twelve years old. They were both among the students who first integrated Terryton's public schools back in the 1960s. Throughout high school, they were often in the same classrooms. But they were not friends during their time in school, only classmates. They developed a friendship years after high school when Eleanor became involved in politics and Michael became a supporter.

"I've heard that there is a new initiative going on in the black community," Eleanor stated. "If you need to know where I heard it, I can certainly tell you that."

"And you would like to know what that new initiative is?" Michael asked.

"Not that I want to judge it or harm it anyway, Michael. I mean, at this point, I don't even know what it is."

"It's not something that's being kept secret, Eleanor. In any case, you and I have this trust thing going on, do we not?"

"Yes, we do, Michael."

"So what do you know so far?" Michael asked.

"Not much, quite frankly."

The server approached the table and asked Eleanor and Michael if they were ready to order. Michael picked up a menu from the table and started to look it over. Eleanor asked the server to give them a few more minutes to decide, and the server stepped away.

Michael began to study the menu. After deciding what he would order, he looked up and noticed that Eleanor was staring at him. He remembered that in the twelfth grade, he sort of had a crush on her. Nothing was ever spoken or acted upon, but he had wondered from time to time whether she had ever had a romantic interest in him.

Michael reached into his briefcase and took out a booklet. "This is for you," he said, delivering the hundred-page booklet to Eleanor. Eleanor read the cover sheet of the booklet and briefly turned a few pages.

"Can I make a copy?" Eleanor asked.

"I have copies here."

Michael reached again into his briefcase and took out three additional copies of the booklet. He put them on the table within Eleanor's reach.

"Michael, does this new initiative or program, for lack of a better word, actually work?"

"It works if you spend the time and do what you're supposed to do," Michael answered. "It's about protecting yourself from the loss of self-esteem and other hurts you may feel on the inside when somebody puts you down or treats you like you're not worth anything. Of course, the self-esteem part is huge."

"Obviously," Eleanor stated. "I can't wait to read it." Looking again at the cover sheet of the booklet, she asked, "Who is the author?"

"Everything you want to know is right there in the booklet," Michael answered.

The server was walking past the table, returning to the kitchen after having served beverages at another table. Eleanor raised her hand and got the server's attention. The server stopped, took lunch orders from Michael and Eleanor and walked away immediately to get the orders filled.

"Don't look now," Eleanor said to Michael, "but there are three men having lunch two tables over to your left. One of those individuals is Sydney Hawkins."

"Really?" Michael asked. "I haven't seen Sydney in years."

"Still selling cars," Eleanor stated. "Though, over the years, in case you don't know, he finds a way to move from one car dealership to another. You never quite know where he is."

Sydney Hawkins had also attended Terryton High School and had graduated in the same class with Eleanor and Michael.

"You never did like him, did you?" Eleanor asked bluntly.

"Sydney and I did have a few fistfights in those days," Michael answered. Immediately, another memory came to his mind, "I believe at one point he was pursuing you to be his girlfriend; am I right? You wouldn't give him the time of day?"

Eleanor smiled. "Why did you not like him, Michael?"

"He had a big mouth, always saying the wrong things."

Eleanor nodded in agreement.

The two friends finished their lunch together that day, promised each other they'd meet again for lunch soon, and went their separate ways.

Eleanor had received a phone call at her home just as she and Zack were finishing an early dinner. She got into her car shortly thereafter and drove directly to Don's house. No question about it, she was agitated. No, she would not call Don beforehand. In her mind, an unannounced visit was precisely what he needed. She would make no apology.

Her initial reaction was to blame herself in part because she felt she could have prevented it. Moments later she reminded herself that she could not anticipate every eventuality. She had given Don a copy of the booklet she received from Michael, and Don had read it. She reasoned that Don must hold himself accountable for behaving in a responsible manner.

Upon arrival, she noticed the different cars at Don's house, some parked in the driveway, and others parked on the street in front of the house. Eleanor parked on the street as well. She got out of her car and walked swiftly up the walkway and onto the well-lighted front porch. She continued to the front door and rang the doorbell. Shortly Don's wife, Cindy, came to the door. At the sight of Eleanor, surprise and alarm registered on her face and in her demeanor. Eleanor explained to Cindy, without hesitation, that she needed to talk to Don immediately and that he should come outside to speak with her privately. Upon hearing this, Cindy returned immediately back into the house.

Soon Don came to the door and walked out onto the porch, closing the door behind him. He stopped and looked directly at Eleanor, who had now taken a seat on the porch bench located a few steps over from the front door.

"I got a call from your sister a short while ago," Eleanor stated. "She was feeling a little uncomfortable about your meeting tonight and wanted to know what I thought about it."

Don moved over and sat down on the bench next to Eleanor. "Claire is always uncomfortable about something, Eleanor, you know that," Don responded. "I don't know why she felt she had to call you."

"I told her I would speak to you," Eleanor answered.

"OK, go ahead and speak. But, before you say anything, what's going on here is not an official meeting or anything like that. I invited some friends over."

"You invited them over for what, Don? To talk?"

"Yes, to talk."

"How many people do you have in there, fifteen, twenty?"

"Look, Eleanor, you're not going to tell me there's something wrong with people getting together to talk about something that's going on in the community."

"Any black people in that meeting, Don? Tell me, did you invite any black people? This is a secret meeting, Don. You invited specific people to your meeting, and none of them is black."

"This is a private gathering, Eleanor. I can invite whomever I choose to talk about whatever we want to talk about," Don asserted angrily.

"You're missing the point," Eleanor answered. "You are the principal of Terryton High School, Don. And when you serve the public as the principal of a high school, you can't secretly organize a bunch of white people to talk about what black folks are doing."

"You're calling this a secret meeting? This is not a secret meeting."

"Ah, come on, Don, it's a secret meeting. You deliberately did not invite black people. Am I right or wrong about that? You deliberately did not invite black people."

"I am not a racist," Don said, with anger still rising. "We have a right to get together to discuss any topic we choose, even if that topic is black people. You can be sure that blacks get together to talk about whites."

Eleanor was concerned about Don's rising level of anger. She certainly wanted to confront him in a forceful manner, but not in a way that would cause him to shut down to what she had to say.

"Don, I am not calling you a racist," Eleanor stated calmly. "I don't mean to say or imply that in any way. You're not a racist."

After a moment of tense silence, Eleanor continued, "Don, we're family. We've always been family, and that's not going to change. I am not here to judge you of anything. I'm here to help, if I can. Now if you want me to get up and walk away right now, I can do that."

"I'm not asking you to leave," Don answered.

"But is that what you want? Do you want me to leave?"

"That's not what I want."

Another moment of silence came upon them during which each reflected privately on their conversation. Shortly, Eleanor started up again, still with calm in her voice.

"Listen to me, Don," she stated, "whether you have the legal right to do what you're doing is not the issue. That's not the point. The point is that a public official such as you, holding a meeting in his home, with black people excluded, to talk about what black people are doing in their lives is not right. It is not helpful, and it's not right. If you want to hold a meeting to talk about what blacks are doing, include black people in your conversation. They are your brothers and sisters, Don. You don't have to talk in secret."

"What I'm feeling right now, Eleanor, is that you don't think I get it," Don stated. "Despite what you believe, I do get it. On the inside, I applaud black people for what they're doing to protect themselves. I fully support it, and I'm actually very excited about it. And I believe that anybody, not just blacks, but anybody who faces bigotry and prejudice can use these same techniques to protect themselves. You see, Eleanor, I *do* get it."

Eleanor understood immediately what Don was saying and knew instantly that he spoke the truth. "I accept that as fair criticism," she responded. "You're absolutely right, I *was* concerned that you didn't get it. But Don, this meeting is not right."

"I guess I've always felt," Don admitted, "that white people should be totally deferential to blacks when talking about issues concerning black people. So I've always felt a bit guarded when talking about racial issues because I didn't want to appear arrogant or offend anybody. It seems you don't have that problem, Eleanor, but does it make sense to you that someone else might feel that way?"

Eleanor nodded her head in the affirmative.

"I want to talk. I wanted to share, but I don't want to offend anybody," Don added.

"You *can* talk, Don," Eleanor responded. "It's all right to talk," she said, "but not in secret. When you talk in secret, people get suspicious. And why wouldn't they? Include black people in your conversations."

Eleanor reached out and took one of Don's hands in hers. "There is no rule," she continued, "against white people talking about what's going on in the lives of their black brothers and sisters. At least, no rule that makes any sense to me. But not in secret, and don't exclude people. If your heart is in the right place, and you do have your heart in the right place, go ahead and talk, but don't exclude people."

Eleanor let go of Don's hand and stood from the bench.

"Are we finished?" Don asked.

"Unless you've got something else on your mind." Eleanor answered.

Don stood. "Yes, I guess I should get back to my guests," he stated.

Eleanor moved across the porch to the walkway.

"What should I say to these people?" Don called out to her. Eleanor waved to Don, without making a verbal response, as if to say to him, "You'll handle it." She continued down the walkway to her car.

Eleanor felt good about her conversation with Don. In her mind, it was a short but very productive encounter. All things considered, she could not have expected a better outcome.

When you see the lie for what it is, the lie dissipates in the wind.

The Dream

————————

I LIVED IN a small town. I don't know where it was, but it was beautiful with seemingly friendly people. I remember walking through a park where some young children were playing on a jungle gym and some teenagers were playing volleyball in front of a small crowd. As I walked on the graveled path through the park, a few fellow walkers waved at me. I had this sense that I really liked this place, and I was glad that I chose to live there.

The next thing I remember is running from gunfire. I think it was another day because the sky was overcast, and I wasn't in the park. I was in the downtown area. I was very scared as I ran behind a brick building with a group of people. We huddled there looking around for the shooter. The weird thing was that we had no idea where the shooter was. There was no one on the street with a gun or anything. It was as if the bullets were coming from the sky. Then I had this thought that there was a sniper somewhere shooting at us. Just as I was looking up around the tops of the buildings for the sniper, a man next to me was shot. I could see his face as he lay on the pavement and struggled to breathe. I told the woman next to me that there was probably a sniper shooting at us. She agreed and told me she saw one on top of the bank and one in the window of a nearby apartment building. I looked around and saw the two dark figures in the places that the woman had pointed out. I thought that if there were two, there were probably more. Even though we were in just as much danger behind the building as we would have been out in the street, we stayed there behind the building. We huddled together and tried to keep the man dying on the street alive for just a little longer. We hoped that help would arrive before it was too late.

I don't know how I got home, but the next part I remember is listening to the news on television. Some time had passed, but I don't know how much, maybe a few weeks. An investigation had been going on about the snipers. The police had estimated that there were four snipers randomly attacking innocent people from the tops of buildings and trees. None of the snipers had been captured, despite the police's efforts. The news report also talked about how people were afraid to leave their homes. No one was going downtown, and there was even talk of canceling school until the snipers were caught so that no children would be shot on their way to school.

Again, I found myself downtown. I was doing some emergency shopping. There were very few people on the street, and I practically ran down the sidewalk toward the grocery store. On my way, I came upon a group of people near the street corner. They were staring at a man that had fallen in the street. Immediately I knew that a sniper had shot him, but people were not as frantic as they should have been. They were just staring at the fallen man. I walked up to the people, assuming that their failure to run meant it was safe.

"What's going on?" I asked, looking at the fallen man.

"The bullets aren't real," a man beside me whispered. I looked at him curiously. "I know it sounds crazy, but look."

He pointed at another man, tall with dark hair, standing on a Dumpster. He had a disassembled gun in his hand. I assumed it was one of the snipers' guns.

"He found one of the guns in that Dumpster over there, and the bullets are made of this putty stuff." I couldn't believe what he was saying. "Go over and look," he told me. I did.

The man had the bullets on display next to him on the Dumpster. They looked as if they were made of Silly Putty. I picked up one and was able to squeeze it between my fingers.

"He's not dead," the man on the Dumpster said. "He wasn't even shot," he continued.

"Then why is he lying there like that?" I asked.

"He thinks he's been shot in the heart, but he couldn't have been. Not with this stuff."

I leaned in to take a closer look. He looked dead. Blood covered his chest. He was pale, and he wasn't breathing.

"Get up!" the man on the Dumpster yelled. "Get up! The bullets aren't real! You're not dead!"

"Are you sure that's what shot him?"

"Yep," he said holding up a smashed piece of putty. "This is what I found on his chest."

"But he's bleeding!" I said.

"Look again," he told me. I looked, and sure enough, the man's white shirt was completely clean when moments ago I had seen it covered in blood. "It's all an illusion," he said to me. "If they only knew the bullets weren't real, all those people wouldn't have died."

"What about him?" I asked.

"If he would just listen to me he won't have to die either."

LIE DETECTIVE

THE CALL CAME in on the police radio. The victim was a black male in his midthirties, and he was down. Sarah Saddlewhite hit the accelerator, passing a cargo van in a no-passing zone. She cut back quickly, barely missing oncoming traffic. Tires squealing, she plunged into the next intersection against a red light and made a sharp left turn onto South Main Street. She stomped the accelerator again and, after a short distance, broke her speed to turn right onto Turners Lane. In the distance, she could see a marked police vehicle with flashing emergency lights parked in the driveway in front of a yellow house. She drove into the driveway and parked her car behind the police cruiser. She got out and rushed into the house.

Sarah Saddlewhite is a lie detective. After graduating from high school, she spent twenty years as an enlisted person doing police work in the military. Joining the city police department after a military career seemed like a natural progression for her. She became a lie detective in particular because, as far back as her girlhood in a small Pennsylvania town, she had always believed in magic. *Everybody's got magic inside*, she silently repeated to herself as she entered the house. *Don't let the lie take your magic away.*

The two police officers on the scene were waiting in the living room as loud voices resonated from the bedroom down the corridor.

Sarah is a tall woman, six feet three inches, with a large body frame. She has big brown eyes, short hair, and a round face. Her physical presence, especially since she is in excellent physical condition, is unforgettable, if not intimidating, to many.

When she entered the bedroom, she could see the man seated in a chair with his eyes focused on the television screen. He was holding a can of beer, and the volume on the television was very high. The sight of "the man down" shook her. Though she had seen it too many times to remember the number, there was never a chance she'd ever get used to it.

She walked over to the man.

"Sir, can you hear me?"

He shifted slightly in his chair but continued to stare at the television.

"I'm here to help you."

He shifted again, picked up the remote control that was on the floor next to him, and turned down the volume on the television.

As the broadcast on the police radio had described, he was indeed a black male in his midthirties. He was of medium build with an angular face and large eyes.

"Are you a cop?" he asked harshly.

"Yes, sir."

"I told those two guys in uniform that I wanted to be left alone."

"I understand that."

"So, what's the problem?"

"The problem is that one of your coworkers called 911. He was concerned when you just walked out of the office without a word."

The man didn't speak. His wife was at work, and his son and daughter were at school.

"I'm here to help you," Sarah repeated.

"How you going to do that?"

"Who did this to you?"

"What difference does it make?"

"It makes a difference."

"I don't see how."

Sarah thought that perhaps he'd been broken. If so, she wanted to get him back as quickly as possible. "Sir, what's your name?" she asked.

"Samuel."

"Samuel, if you tell me what happened to you, I think I can help. No promises, but I want to try to help you."

Samuel was impressed that Sarah had called him "Samuel." He didn't like it when people assumed it was OK to call him "Sam." He muted the television.

"You want me to tell you what happened?" Samuel asked.

"I need to know the facts."

"Where do I start?"

"Just talk to me."

"Did you know I work at the motor vehicle department?"

"I didn't know that, sir."

Sarah didn't push. She just waited in silence. It turned out to be a longer-than-expected silence before Samuel began to talk freely. He was a bit too random in Sarah's opinion. Nevertheless, she listened intently as he told her that his unit manager was black and that some of his co-workers didn't think she deserved the position. There was tension in the office. At about nine-thirty in the morning, he went to get some papers signed. When he returned, he found this "thing" just lying there right in the middle of his desk.

"Sir, what thing are you talking about?" Sarah interrupted.

"It was a white sheet of paper with some words scribbled on it."

"And what did the words say?" Sarah asked with a bit of impatience.

"It said 'Black People' equal 'Stupid', and the 'equal' was like the equal sign," Samuel explained.

"Black people equal stupid?"

"Yeah, with the equal sign." Samuel paused for a moment as if to give Sarah time to reflect on what he had told her. "At first, you know, I was like, 'I can't believe it," he continued, "and then I started to get angry. I wanted to know who would do something like that, and I started to look around at my coworkers at their desks. Our desks are out in this open area, and I could see everybody."

"What did you do with the piece of paper," Sarah asked.

"I gave it to my manager. They'll probably do an investigation, but that's going to amount to nothing."

"Sir, why do you say that?"

"I mean first they'll have to find out who did it, but how're they going to do that? And even if they do, not much is going to happen."

"Samuel," Sarah began, "I have something to tell you, and I want you to listen to me very carefully. Do you understand?"

"Yeah, I'm listening."

"It was a lie, Samuel. You have to understand that. It was all a lie."

"I don't know what you're talking about. You mean what was on the paper, that black people are stupid? I know that's a lie."

"Not just what was written on the paper but the whole thing. Whenever somebody tries to put you down, they're saying you are not as worthy as other people, and that's the lie I'm talking about."

"OK, it's a lie. So what?" Samuel asked.

"Then treat it as if it's a lie. When somebody tells you a lie, don't you ever forget that what you're dealing with is not true and never will be true," Sarah replied.

"I hear what you're saying, but what good is it? You say it's a lie. Well, I know it's a lie," Samuel said.

"But did you call it a lie?"

"You mean, out loud?"

"In whatever way you choose."

"No, I never called it a lie."

"You have to call it a lie, Samuel. Do you understand?"

"I hear you. But, like I said, what good is it?"

"It makes a difference when you know you're dealing with a lie. When you remember you're dealing with a lie, the lie doesn't hurt you on the inside like it used to. What I'm telling you, Samuel, is that you have the power to liberate yourself from the lie. 'Black people equal stupid' is a lie. It's nothing but a lie, Samuel. Does that make sense to you?"

"What kind of cop are you?"

Sarah took a business card from her jacket and handed it to him. "I'm a lie detective. I investigate the lie."

Samuel read the card and then stared at Sarah with a puzzled look on his face.

"The lie we just discussed," Sarah continued, "I investigate that lie wherever it might be. Sir, do you understand what I'm saying to you?"

"Maybe," Samuel answered.

"I need you to understand me."

"Right now I just want to be left alone. I want to be by myself if you don't mind." Samuel pressed a button on his remote control, and there was sound again from the television.

Sarah asked herself at that point the very question every lie detective must ask and answer when called to a scene: *Is the victim ready?* Sarah felt that Samuel wasn't ready. She heard it in his voice; she saw it in his eyes. He was not resistant, and she had seen her share of resistance. But he was not open or receptive either. Perhaps one day he would be, but not today. She had sympathy for him, but she saw no value in pushing against the wind.

"Sir," she said to him, "I'm sorry to have taken up your time."

"I just want to be alone. You can understand that, can't you?" Samuel offered.

Sarah nodded, turned, and left the room. Samuel reread Sarah's business card and dropped it on the floor. He turned the volume on the television back up to its highest level. He took a sip of beer and stared at the television screen.

When someone comes after you, foaming at the mouth, go ahead and protect yourself at all times, but remember it's not you but the person foaming at the mouth who's got the problem.

Liars Anonymous

JOHN EVERGREEN IS forty-five years old, tall and skinny, with a bit of gray in his dark thinning hair. He is pleasant and well suited to teach social science at the high-school level, which is precisely what he does. He lives alone, and, on the particular evening in question, he had pizza for dinner before settling in to watch television. At about nine-thirty, he received a phone call from Carol and immediately got into his car and drove over to her house.

This was probably a mistake, Carol thought as she sat across the kitchen table from John. Carol is also forty-five years old, just two months older than John. She is slightly overweight, medium height, with short blond hair and a round face. When she called John earlier, she told him she needed to talk. She didn't tell him what she wanted to discuss, and he didn't insist on knowing.

As they sat at the table, she wondered if he felt "put upon." She asked him about it outright, and he told her he didn't mind coming over. But she wasn't sure if he was being truthful. She started talking about this and that, like what she saw on television or what she read in the newspaper, and they both knew she was just passing time in her anxiety. She kept up the chatter for a while until she was ready. Then she began telling him what happened that evening when she went out to dinner with two of her coworkers.

"One thing led to another," she explained, "and we ended up telling lies right there in the restaurant."

John was silent, and Carol could tell from his silence and how he looked away, avoiding eye contact, that he was judging her. She wasn't surprised but still disappointed. She had hoped he would be more supportive.

"John, it happened," Carol said. "That's about all I can say right now; it just happened."

"But how did it happen?"

"Like I said, one thing led to another."

"But one thing led to another does not equal lying."

"I've gone over it, over and over in my head," Carol said. "And I don't have an explanation. I'm certainly not trying to defend what I've done."

"Well, at least you've got that going for you."

"I don't need you to be sarcastic, John," Carol responded. "By the way, I know some of the disparaging things we were saying, about Puerto Ricans in particular, were true."

"How can you say that?" John asked with a bit of irritation in his voice.

"What do you mean?"

"When you state or imply someone is inferior," John answered, "it's a lie just like any other lie. That's your problem, Carol. You want to make a distinction. There is no distinction. A lie is a lie."

John and Carol had lived together in marriage for a period of fifteen years. During the marriage, each experienced a loss of romantic interest. This development in their relationship occurred gradually over a period of time, and neither could say precisely when or how it happened. But for sure it did happen, and they made up their minds to go their separate ways. However, they still managed to maintain a good relationship in part for the benefit of their daughter who was now away at college. They also trusted each other and genuinely cared for one another. Carol knew that she could rely on John and that ultimately he would be there for her whenever she needed him.

"So, what am I going to do?" she asked.

"What do you mean 'what're you going to do'?"

"I mean, how do I handle this thing?"

"You obviously handle it by never doing it again."

"But I have to deal with what has already happened."

Yeah, that's also a problem, John thought. Carol was a real-estate agent with a strong interest in local politics. She initially got involved in politics when her daughter was in middle school. At that time, it was an avenue to express her concern that the state was not spending enough on public education. Later, she got involved in other issues as well. John was always supportive of Carol in her political ambitions but doubted whether she had the toughness to run as a candidate for political office. He saw her role primarily as a behind-the-scenes worker. But some members of the Democratic town committee had recently asked her if she had an interest in being a candidate for the state general assembly in the upcoming election. She was excited about the possibility. Now, however, if the word got out that she had been lying, especially in a public place like a restaurant, it would ruin her chances not only of getting elected but also of getting the Democratic nomination in the first place.

"Don't worry about it," John said. "It's over. I mean, how is anybody to know?"

"John," Carol said as she leaned forward and dropped her voice. "Quinn Taylor was in the restaurant."

The revered Quinn Taylor! If Carol succeeded in getting the Democratic nomination, she would face Taylor, the incumbent, in the general election.

"When we got up to leave," Carol continued, "I saw him and another man and a woman sitting at the next table. I didn't know he was there. Obviously, if I knew he was there, I wouldn't have been sitting at the table telling lies. He must have come in after we were seated. I had my back to his table, and I just never noticed he was there."

"Did you talk to him?" John asked.

"No, I didn't talk to him. Under the circumstances, I wasn't going to talk to him," Carol answered angrily. She then took a deep breath. "But we did walk past his table on the way out. He didn't make eye contact, and that was that."

"And you're assuming he overheard you lying?"

"That would be the assumption. We certainly weren't whispering."

"But you're not sure?"

"No, I'm not sure," Carol said. "He was close enough to hear us, I think, and he certainly knows who I am, but, to tell you the truth, I just don't know."

Carol had been dealing with the problem of lying throughout her entire life. With outside support, she had been doing fine for a number of years. The last time she spoke to John about it, she told him she was clear and that the problem had been finally resolved. She was embarrassed to have had to tell him she had taken a step backward.

John got up from the table to get something to drink. "You know, if he comes out in public with this thing, you can always deny it," he stated, pouring a glass of orange juice for himself from the refrigerator.

"I wouldn't do that," Carol said. "Besides, there were two witnesses, and I just wouldn't do that."

"I'm just trying to lay out the alternatives," John answered.

"You don't think I should tell the Town Committee, do you?"

Now why would you do that? John thought, but he did not say it. Instead, he asked her if she wanted some juice, and she shook her head no. "Don't tell the Town Committee," John stated, settling back into his seat.

"I have to," Carol responded.

"Why?"

"It would be a deception. You know it would be a deception if I didn't tell them."

Carol was irritated that John apparently had no difficulty with the issue. He had always been the one to preach integrity.

"I'm not going to let them get blindsided by this whole thing," she snapped.

"Who says they're going to get blindsided?" John asked. "At this point, you don't know for sure if Quinn Taylor heard anything at all. You shouldn't be the one putting this thing out there. There's no reason to sabotage your campaign. Think about it, Carol. You made a mistake. That's what we're talking about here, a mistake—a stupid mistake, but still a mistake."

Carol got up from the table. "It's bigger than a mistake, and you know that." Without saying anything more, she left the kitchen and entered the living room. John gulped down his orange juice and followed.

John realized Carol needed to talk, and he was committed to be there to listen. Beyond that, he felt he had nothing to offer her. She got caught lying, and that was a major problem for her. He was not going to pretend otherwise. And his suggestion about not telling the Town Committee was just that: a suggestion. It was her decision all the way. She was the one who'd have to deal with the consequences. He wasn't trying to run her life, and he hoped she understood that.

Carol was lying on the living room couch under a blanket. Clearly, at this point, she wanted to be alone.

"I'll call you later," John said as walked toward the front door.

"Don't worry about it. It's not your problem."

"I said I'll call you later."

"Whatever."

John left the house.

At the First Baptist Church downtown on Elm Street, in the meeting room downstairs on the basement floor, a candle flickered on the table up-front as soft music played in the background. Preston, a huge black man in his early fifties, with a shaved head and peppered moustache, was sitting in a chair next to the table. He faced the audience, about twenty-five people in total, as they sat quietly in the calm, serene atmosphere. Carol walked into the room, found a seat near the back, and took a deep breath to relax her body. She wasn't sure, but she thought

Preston noticed her when she came in. She felt it would be good to talk to him—so good to talk, and so very important.

Carol realized she needed to get help, and after some deliberation, she decided to attend at least one meeting. One meeting was a risk she was willing to take. Whether she would continue after that was another matter.

As a possible candidate for the general assembly, Carol was concerned that attending the meetings would raise an issue of her fitness to hold public office. She felt people in general were genuinely forgiving of liars for past behavior, but not so much for continuing offenses. Even if she could keep the incident about telling lies in the restaurant private, attending Liars Anonymous meetings would convince some she was currently struggling. She did not want to do anything further to threaten her political opportunities.

Preston shut off a CD player and stood. He broke the silence by introducing himself. "My name is Preston, and I'm a liar," he said, his deep voice resonating throughout the room. He then extended a welcome to everyone. "This meeting is for you," he continued. "We have come together this evening not to judge one another or to impose ourselves on one another in any way, but to share and support each other in our individual struggles for liberation."

For fourteen years, Carol had attended the meetings on a regular basis. She had initially entered the program as most others did, because she was sinking low and had no other place to turn. She stayed because the meetings had helped her to grow and because she was afraid that without them she would slip back into darkness. During her time in the program, she worked hard on her feelings of insecurity, and her fear of relapse faded over time. Eighteen months earlier, she had found herself at the point where she believed she no longer needed the meetings, and she just stopped attending. Still, it was tough to let go. She sorely missed the people in the program.

Carol looked around the room and saw familiar faces: Carla who talked so fast it was difficult to understand her, James the firefighter who had once gotten into a shoving match with Preston, and Andrea, the most senior person in the group, who had such warmth that it was difficult to imagine she was a liar. There were unfamiliar faces as well, among them a young man sitting just four seats away, with long hair in a ponytail and the tattoo of a cobra on his right arm. Carol noticed him in particular, not so much because of his rugged appearance, but because he appeared to be in his early twenties, about the same age as her daughter. Though she did not know the particulars of the young man's situation, she had immediate sympathy for him. She wanted to know the extent of his dependency on lying and what support, if any, he was receiving from his friends and family.

Preston continued to speak to those in attendance, now asking various questions about lying in an effort to get group participation in a discussion. The regulars responded, some answering the questions presented and raising other questions of their own. Some just offered advice on how to live better lives. In the past, Carol would have participated in the discussion as well, but tonight due to her ambivalence about coming back to the program, she decided just to listen.

She looked over again at the young man with the ponytail. He was now slouched in his chair with his eyes closed. Those around him pretended not to notice, including the man with red hair sitting next to him.

The man with red hair, a new attendee in his mid thirties, stood and faced the group. "My name is Jamie, and I'm a liar," he stated to everyone. He then began to talk about lies he had told in the past. Meanwhile, the young man with the ponytail remained slouched in his chair, eyes still closed, still seemingly uninterested in what anyone had to say.

Every liar has a story, and Carol is no exception. The first lie she remembers telling was when she was in the third grade. It happened on the playground at school. She called her classmate Mia "nigger" and then huddled with her friends, and together they giggled among themselves because the lie made them feel good. They were giddy.

Carol continued to lie throughout her childhood, making disparaging comments and otherwise demeaning others, whenever she felt like it, although not on a daily basis. She was afflicted with her own false sense that she was better than certain people. But she wasn't a hateful person. In general, she was friendly even to those who were different, except when she felt compelled to act on her bigotry.

In her junior year of high school, she began to change. Her English teacher, Mrs. Elfman, for whom she had great respect, was a strong advocate of the principle that everyone, no matter who they are, has value. Mrs. Elfman personally challenged Carol to make a commitment to grow out of her dependency on lying, and Carol responded. In her sophomore year in college, when she met her future husband John, she had evolved to the point where she had little tolerance for the lie or anyone who embraced it. All was well for the time being, but later, as a young working mother, she got caught once again in the trap of lying. A black man at the utilities company where she worked was promoted. Carol felt he was promoted only because he was black and that the promotion should have been given to her. She reacted with anger and resentment against all black people. She knew it was wrong to feel that way and struggled to change her attitude. John was supportive, though she felt he looked down on her, if ever so slightly, because of her affliction. Fortunately for Carol, a coworker named Janet befriended her at that time and directed her to Liars Anonymous.

When the meeting ended, no one left the church. Instead, all lingered for conversation, some speaking to friends and acquaintances and others just meeting for the first time. Only one person did not stay to chat with others: the young man with the ponytail. Carol watched as he got up from his seat and made his way through the attendees toward the door. Despite his lack of interest, Carol wanted to reach out to him, but she had to get to him before he walked out. She started to move toward him, but James approached her, extending pleasantries and saying he had missed her and that it was good to see her again. She didn't dislike

James, but she wasn't particularly fond of him either. She thought he was a bit of a showman. She would promptly excuse herself and continue on her way. But before she could do so, with James still in her face, she noticed that Preston was now talking to the young man. That being the case, she felt she could probably tolerate James for just a moment or two longer. She thanked him for his "kind words" and stated further that it was good to see everyone again.

Before Carol could break off her conversation with James, Preston came over with his arms open. Carol walked into his embrace, and he held her in a big hug. He then released her, and they looked into each other's eyes. Yes, she had missed his infectious smile.

"Hello, stranger," he said.

"I'm no stranger."

"That's for sure."

Unobtrusively, James walked away.

"What I think I needed more than anything else was that hug," Carol said.

Preston and Carol had started the Liars Anonymous program at about the same time. Preston had a long history of lying himself, which included some acts of violence. From different worlds and different perspectives, he and Carol were combatants in the beginning as they worked through troubling issues. Later, they developed a mutual respect for one another. This respect transformed into a deep friendship, most evident when Carol turned to Preston as a confidant during her struggle with the breakdown of her marriage.

"I hope things have been going well for you," Preston said.

"As well as one could expect, I guess I could say, except, that's not the truth. Actually, Preston, I really screwed up."

"Ah, it can't be that bad."

"I'm so disappointed in myself."

"You know what? You can fix it. There's nothing so broke you can't fix it."

"Some things are."

"Well, there aren't many, at least in my opinion," Preston said. He then took Carol's hand in his. "Maybe we won't get a chance to talk tonight, but let's talk. You'll have to make it so. You know how to reach me."

"I will," Carol answered.

Preston glanced back briefly at the young man with the ponytail. "I promised to give this gentleman a ride home, so he wouldn't have to catch the bus."

"I noticed him earlier."

"Look, let me introduce you."

The young man had taken a seat and didn't rise as Carol and Preston approached.

"Adam, I'd like you to meet my friend. This is Carol," Preston said.

"Hello, Adam," Carol said extending her hand.

Adam reached out and shook Carol's hand loosely, without making eye contact.

"Are all the people here liars?" Adam asked.

Preston glanced briefly around the room. "As a matter of fact, they are."

"You, too? What's a black guy like you doing being a liar?"

"It doesn't matter who you are," Preston said. "And by the way, I don't tell lies anymore; at least I don't think I do. But I used to. It's like this: once a liar, always a liar. Right now, I'm a liar in recovery. These folks here are in recovery too, at least most of them."

"What are you doing here, Adam, if you don't mind my asking?" Carol said. "It seems you'd rather be someplace else."

"The judge sent me. It's part of my probation."

"What kind of trouble did you get yourself into?"

"I broke into the house of these black folks and stole something."

"And I assume you did it because they're black?"

"Yeah," Adam answered as if it was no big deal.

Neither Carol nor Preston got excited about his response. They had seen it before, and they had certainly been in unhealthy places themselves.

"Obviously, you don't like black people," Carol said, "and now you expect Preston to give you a ride home?"

"Look, lady. I didn't ask him. He came over here to me."

"Do you hate black people?"

"What's it to you?"

"I ask because I care about you."

"You care about black folks. I can see that."

"I also care about you."

"You don't even know me, lady."

At that point, Carol shut up and stopped asking questions. She was concerned. *This boy is lost*, she thought. *I don't know if anybody can ever get through to him.*

"Let's go," Preston said to the young man, "I'll give you that ride now."

Preston then made eye contact with Carol. "We'll talk," he said to her as a reminder. She nodded, and Preston started walking toward the door. Adam followed.

Carol was running late. She had a house across town to show in an hour and had lost track of time doing catch-up paperwork. She shuffled through the piles of papers on her desk, located a missing form, and held it up like a prize. When she raised her eyes, she noticed a man standing in the doorway of her office.

"Preston," she said, rising promptly from her seat.

"Mind if I come in?" he asked, stepping further into the office. "You know, I was prepared to bribe my way past your receptionist, but she remembered me."

"She wouldn't forget you."

There was a moment of uneasy silence. Carol then looked at the clock on the wall more as a signal to Preston than for her own information. "You've caught me at a bad time," she said, looking at the clock again.

"Oh, I understand you're busy," he said. "This will only take a minute."

"Preston, I was going to get back to you. I was all freaked out. I thought I had a chance to run for a seat in the General Assembly. But when I told the Town Committee about my baggage, that was it."

"What baggage are you talking about? You don't mean Liars Anonymous?"

"I screwed up, Preston. I'll have to tell you about that."

"So, what's up now? I mean, is it all over?"

"Yeah, but that's OK. I'm all right with it. Look, Preston, I know I should have gotten back to you. I had my head buried in my own self-pity."

"I didn't come over here to put any pressure on you to talk," Preston answered. "I hope you don't think that's the case. Whenever you want to talk about something, you make that decision. It's always been up to you."

Carol knew he spoke the truth.

"I'm here about Adam."

"Adam?"

"The young man at the meeting."

"Yes, Adam."

"He was asking about you at the meeting last night. It seems you've connected with him."

"That surprises me. You saw the resistance."

"It's a mask for the fear."

"I suppose so."

This time Preston glanced at the clock. "Look, I said 'a minute,' and that's what I meant. I'm not going to interfere with your work." He turned and started for the door.

"Preston," Carol called quickly. He stopped and faced her. She wanted to say more but understood it couldn't be now. "Thanks for coming by," she said to him. He nodded and walked out of the door.

Soon Carol was in her car driving to meet her clients across town. She knew it was no small matter that Preston visited her in her office. He was fighting for Adam, and to know he was doing so was an inspiration to her. She had been so focused on taking care of herself that she hadn't given enough consideration lately to helping others. She had forgotten what was taught in the program, that Liars Anonymous was not only for receiving, but also for giving. She had forgotten that her mere presence at the meetings could serve to help others even in ways she'd never know.

Carol stopped at a red light and watched bumper-to-bumper cars and trucks make their way through the intersection in front of her. Traffic was heavy, too heavy to make it to her clients on time. She took a deep breath to calm herself. The light turned green, and traffic began to move quicker than she expected. She drove into the intersection. She would still be late, but only by five or ten minutes.

Up a Tree

DAN CHAMBERS IS a big man, six feet four in height, weighing about 240. He turned fifty-five in January and looks good for a man of his age and physical stature. He lives with his wife in Connecticut and is employed as a supervisor at the state's department of labor. He was on the highway in his pickup truck, driving home from work in busy but fast-moving traffic. He found himself in the center lane, wanting to take the next exit coming up immediately on his left. He noticed three or four speeding cars, one behind the other, in the left lane where he had to be to take the exit. "Son of gun! I can't get over," he thought. He should have moved over earlier; he knew the traffic pattern, and it was his own fault for not paying attention. "All things considered, it's no big deal," he reasoned. He stayed in the middle lane and accepted the reality that he would have to take exit twenty, a longer route home but really not that bad.

Shortly he took exit twenty on the right without a problem. He turned left at the end of the ramp onto Hubbard Road, drove five minutes down Hubbard, took a right onto Cedar, went down Cedar to the traffic light, and then took another right onto Colby Street.

Colby Street runs through a residential area of single homes. It has one lane for traffic in each direction with no room for parking on either side. There's moderate traffic on Colby Street at different times during the day because some town residents use this route to get to the highway.

Shortly after turning onto Colby Street, Dan noticed a man in a tree on the lawn of the yellow house on his right. He slowed down immediately to get a better look.

Is that a man up a tree? he thought. *That can't be a man up a tree!* He wanted to stop to make certain he was seeing what he was seeing, but there was a car following behind and also cars approaching in the opposite direction.

Dan continued to drive slowly as he examined further to see what was going on. Suddenly, his mind was racing.

Yeah, that's a man up a tree, for sure. And I don't see a saw in his hands or anything like that. So he's certainly not doing any tree-trimming. Sightseeing? Don't tell me that. Yeah, that's a man up a tree.

Dan was driving so slowly that he had almost come to a stop on the road. The woman following in the car behind him sounded her horn. Dan sped up and turned right onto the first side street a short distance ahead. He drove down the side street for another short distance and stopped his pickup in the right lane. There was no place off the travel portion of the road to park, except on somebody's lawn, and Dan would certainly not do that. He felt he was OK where he was. Any approaching traffic could safely steer around his pickup. In any case, he would be there only a short period of time.

He sat there for a moment in his pickup reflecting on the situation. He wanted to walk back to Colby Street and take another look at that man up the tree. He felt he had gotten a pretty good look as he drove by, but he couldn't tell for sure if the man had any rocks in his possession. Perhaps he had some rocks in his pockets. Dan stepped out of the pickup, and as he was about to walk back in the direction of Colby Street, he noticed something moving in yet another tree on the front lawn of a white house on the very side street where he was standing. He felt obliged to investigate further and walked in the direction of the white house. He stopped when he had a good and clear view of what was going on.

He saw a woman dressed in business attire in a tree on the front lawn of the white house. She was wearing a dress and nylons. She was not wearing shoes probably because shoes would have impeded her climb. She had her purse on her shoulder, and Dan speculated that she had rocks in that purse. Dan looked carefully at the woman.

Yes, he thought. *No tree-trimming here. No sightseeing either. What we have here is a woman up a tree.* Dan stared at the woman. The woman stared back. He did not confront her. He would leave confrontation, if at all, for another time and place. He simply backed away and got back into his vehicle.

Minutes later, Dan drove into the driveway of his longtime friend Lenny Talbot. Lenny was on his lawn tractor, mowing his lawn. Dan got out of his pickup, walked onto the lawn, and waited as Lenny approached on the tractor. When Lenny reached Dan, he shut down the engine on the tractor and took off his earplugs.

"Can I talk to you for a minute?" Dan called out.

"You just getting home?" Lenny asked.

"I didn't go home yet."

"What's up?"

Dan took a deep breath, "I saw a man up a tree—over on Colby Street, near the intersection with Cedar."

Lenny stepped down from the tractor. "Are you sure?" he asked.

"And he wasn't sightseeing or trimming limbs or anything like that," Dan responded. "I'm telling you it was a man up a tree."

After reflecting for a moment on what he was hearing, Lenny answered, "That is so disappointing. Right here in town? I hate to see it anywhere, but right here in our town?"

"Disappointing. You said 'disappointing.' That's exactly what I'm feeling."

"Which house, was it, Dan? It did happen at a house, right?"

"That yellow house, right near the intersection. You know the house I'm talking about."

"Yeah, I know that house. A new family moved in there about six months ago. Bob Carter used to live there."

"I don't know any of them."

Lenny is a lifelong resident of the town in which he and Dan live except for the four years he was away in the military after graduating from high school. He met Dan for the first time at a town meeting twenty-five years ago, shortly after Dan and his family moved into the community.

Lenny is heavily involved in local politics. He served on various town boards and town committees over the years. Ten years prior he ran for first selectman and lost by only fifty votes. He is currently serving on the town's board of finance.

"It's disgusting, man. Just downright disgusting," Lenny offered.

"I have to tell you," Dan added, "that right after I saw the man I'm telling you about, I saw a woman up a tree at another house."

"Is this some kind of joke?" Lenny asked firmly.

"Lenny, I wouldn't joke about this."

Lenny looked into Dan's eyes and could see the sadness there.

"And no," Dan continued, "she was not sightseeing or tree-trimming or anything like that. She was up a tree. I got a good look at her."

"And where did you see her?" Lenny asked.

"On that side street right after the yellow house," Dan answered. "After I saw the man up the tree," he continued, "I turned down that side street because I wanted to stop and get a better look. And boom, there she was. Up a tree, right in front of my own eyes."

"That side street you're talking about is Seal Street," Lenny explained.

"I don't care. She was up a tree. Is there anything we can do about it?" Dan asked.

"Like what?"

"I don't know. Hold a town meeting or something?"

"Sure, we can bring it up at the next town meeting, but what good is that gonna do? It's not against the law to climb a tree."

Dan looked away in frustration.

"Look, Dan, I'm not saying we should do nothing. We'll keep doing what we're doing, trying to help people change. But change takes time. For this day right here in front of us, there's just so much you can do."

Dan reflected for a moment on what he was hearing. "You speak the truth, Lenny, the whole truth," Dan replied. "Look, you've got work to do. I've kept you long enough. Thank you for listening."

Dan started walking away toward his pickup. Lenny watched for a moment and then called out, "Look, I'll ask around to see if I can find out something about those folks." Without stopping, Dan waved to acknowledge he had heard Lenny's comments, and he continued on his way. Lenny climbed back onto his tractor, put the earplugs back on, and started the engine.

Shortly, Dan entered the driveway at his home on Day Street. His daughter's car was parked there, and this pleased him. He enjoys her frequent visits. Her name is Mattie. She works in the claims department of an insurance company and lives in an apartment thirty minutes away. Dan parked next to her car, mindful to not block her in. He got out of his pickup and entered the living room through the front door.

Dan's wife, Susan, was seated on the couch, and Mattie was seated in a chair across from her.

"Hi, honey," Susan greeted her husband.

"Hi, baby," Dan responded, walking over to Susan. He gave her a kiss on the cheek.

Mattie stood from her seat. "Hi, Daddy."

Dan moved over to Mattie and gave her a hug.

"How you doing, baby girl?"

"Fine."

Dan noticed that Susan had a pad and pen in her hands. "What are you guys up to?" he asked.

"How was work, Daddy?" Mattie asked, ignoring Dan's question for the moment. She sat back down in the chair.

"Work was OK," Dan answered.

"Just OK?" Susan asked.

"Yeah, it was OK."

Susan is the office manager at a local orthopedic medical practice. She and Dan have two children, their son Robert, the older of the two, lives in Maryland with his wife Denise. Robert and Denise are both teachers in the public school system.

"But there is something I need to tell you," Dan added. "Not work-related, but I need to tell you."

"Something private?" Susan asked.

"You mean in front of Mattie? We don't keep secrets from Mattie… Well, not many."

"Is it something you need to tell me right now, at this very moment?"

"At this very moment? No, not at this very moment."

"Then sit with us. Can you spend a little time sitting with us?"

"What's that you've got written on the pad?" Dan asked, taking a seat on the couch next to Susan.

Susan gave the pad to Dan. "It's a list of the people coming to the cookout on Saturday, including what everybody is bringing." Dan took a cursory look at the names and items written on the pad.

"Anything on that list stand out to you, Daddy?" Mattie asked. Dan started to read over the list again, this time with focus.

"Should I be looking for something in particular?" Dan asked.

"Cousin Charlie," Susan answered. "Cousin Charlie is on the list. Are you OK with that?"

Dan took a moment and located Cousin Charlie's name on the list. "Why wouldn't I be OK with that?"

"Well, that's good," Susan replied, "because I have already invited him."

Charlie is Susan's first cousin. By occupation, he is an electrician. He had married and lived in California for over twenty-five years with his wife and two children born of their marriage. After the children went away to college, Charlie's marriage broke down. He moved back east to the state of his birth and ended up living in a condo in the next town over from Dan and Susan.

Dan and Susan had seen Charlie at different times over the years at weddings and funerals and on other occasions when he and his family would visit from California. Dan and Susan understand clearly that Charlie is a different kind of person. He is friendly enough, no question about that, but at times he speaks without thinking. He says inappropriate things at the most inappropriate times. He tells jokes that aren't funny. He often postures or performs in the presence of others in an effort to be the sole focus of attention.

"Dad, we wanted to ask you to sort of keep a watch over Cousin Charlie, you know, while he's at the cookout," Mattie stated.

Dan reflected for a moment. "Now, when you say keep a watch, you mean—"

"Just keep him from being inappropriate, Dan. You know what we mean," Susan interrupted.

"And just how am I supposed to do that?" Dan protested. "In my opinion, *nobody* can keep Charlie from being inappropriate."

"Just do the best you can, Dad," Mattie answered. "Most of all don't let him start doing that stupid dance. You know, that Shuka Bacca dance where he's just jumping all around and stuff."

Dan chuckled out loud.

"I wouldn't invite him, but he's family. He needs to be around family. He's been through a lot," Susan argued.

"The best that anyone can do with Cousin Charlie is try," Dan answered.

"I understand that," Susan responded.

Dan looked over at Mattie and then back to Susan, "I'll do my best, that's all I can do."

"Thank you."

"Thank you, Daddy. You're a good man," Mattie added.

Dan and Susan had parked their own vehicles in the garage before guests started arriving. By midafternoon, eight cars were tightly parked in their driveway and six additional cars were parked on the street in front of their house. Mattie had arrived early to assist her parents as needed. Dan's brother, Mike, was the next arrival, along with his wife, Betty, and their six-year-old granddaughter, Michelle. Michelle's parents were out of town for the weekend. Moments later, Cousin Charlie arrived with his usual high level of energy. Mattie made eye contact with her father as if to say, "You know what you have to do."

Susan's siblings, Debby, Claire, and Marvin, arrived along with their spouses. Debby, Claire, and Marvin had a combined total of nine children, and some of their children had spouses and children themselves, but not all came to the cookout. Susan's nieces and nephews at the cookout, together with their spouses and children, included six adults, two teenagers, and six children ranging in ages from three to twelve.

Susan's niece, Myra, invited a couple that came to the cookout with their eight-year-old son. Susan invited a friend, also named Betty, who attended with her two daughters, one age seven and the other age twelve. Marvin invited Nate, a recently divorced coworker. The next-door neighbor to Dan and Susan attended with their two children, ages five and seven. Mattie's boyfriend, James, came but stayed only for an hour or so. He had to leave early to go to the airport and pick up his parents, who had been visiting friends in South Carolina.

Before disaster struck, it was a festive day indeed in all things. Guests were moving around and about on the premises, in and out of the house, back and forth on the deck and lawn, engaged in different activities and generally enjoying themselves. Two of Susan's adult nephews were on the front lawn near the maple tree, playing ball with two young boys. The boys were taking turns hitting a plastic ball with a plastic bat. One nephew was pitching, and the other was running down the balls that were hit.

Four other children were running about on the lawn in a game of tag. Betty, Mike's wife, was relaxing on the hammock under the shade of a tree at the edge of the lawn. Two adults were setting up a game on the back lawn.

Debby was on the deck cooking hamburger patties on the gas grill. A table on the deck was occupied with chips, salsa, paper plates, paper cups, plastic utensils, and other picnic items. Chairs were in place for guests to sit. Two umbrellas, each supported by a base, were on the deck as well, strategically placed to provide relief from the sun.

A large picnic table covered with a tablecloth was on the lawn near the deck, loaded with hamburger rolls, hot-dog rolls, condiments, and other food items for the taking. Two coolers filled with ice and an assortment of beverages were next to the table. Off at a distance, Susan's brother-in-law, Sal, was cooking hot dogs on a small charcoal grill. Five adults were seated in lawn chairs under a portable canopy, talking sports, politics, and other events, and catching up on the positive things that different family members were doing with their lives.

Dan was in the basement of the house examining the contents of storage containers that were stacked near the foot of the stairs. He was searching for a plastic bag of loose photographs that he had previously stored in one of the containers. The photographs captured individuals and activities of family cookouts in past years. Being together with family and friends that day, Dan was feeling especially grateful for the people in his life, and wanted to share the photographs, at the appropriate time, as an expression of the sense of community he was feeling.

After a bit of searching, Dan located the photographs, set them aside, and started to put the storage containers back in place. Suddenly, he heard what sounded like Mattie's excited voice calling him from a distance. He listened. In a moment, he clearly heard Mattie shouting to him from the top of the basement stairs.

"Daddy! Daddy!"

"I'm here, Mattie. What is it?"

"Daddy, he's up the tree!"

"What?" Dan questioned, in disbelief.

"He's up the tree, Daddy. I'm telling you, he's up the tree."

Dan dropped everything and rushed onto the stairs. In haste, he stumbled on the stairs and went down, banging the right leg just below the knee. He was up immediately and continued quickly up the stairs, across the kitchen floor, out onto the deck, and then onto the lawn.

Guests were standing on the lawn looking up into the maple tree. Dan was totally confused. Cousin Charlie was not in the tree but among the others who were standing there looking up. Dan moved closer to get a better view.

Marvin's coworker, Nate, was halfway up the tree, and had settled there, holding himself tightly in place. Marvin was standing at the foot of the tree, trying to talk Nate down, but Nate was not responding.

Dan moved over and stood next to Marvin, "What's going on?"

"I don't know," Marvin answered, "He's up the tree."

"You didn't see it coming?"

Marvin shakes his head, "And he's got a bad back, too."

"Physical limitations won't keep anybody out of the tree."

"I understand that," Marvin agreed.

Nate shifted a bit in the tree to more securely fix himself in his location.

"Mind if I talk to him?" Dan asked Marvin.

"Not at all. If you can help, that would be great."

Dan shuffled a bit on the ground to put himself in the best position to have a clear view of Nate, and for Nate to have a clear view of him as well.

"Nate, I know you can hear me," Dan offered. "I want to ask you something. Why are you up there in that tree?"

Dan's brother, Mike, who was standing nearby, interjected with agitation, "Why are you asking him why he's up the tree? You know why he's up that tree!"

"Uncle Dan," a young girl shouted out, "What's wrong with the man?" The young girl's mother whispered in the youngster's ear.

Dan looked around at the children who were standing there focused on what was going on. No one would dare send the children away. Everyone understood that the children especially needed to witness the occasion to strengthen them on the inside.

Dan turned his attention back to the man up the tree. "Nate, you're up in a tree, do you understand me? That's what happens when you go down the wrong path. You have compromised yourself. You're up a tree.

Everybody knows what's going on here. You're scared that if you're not better than other people, you're not worth much of anything yourself."

Nate looked down directly at Dan. Dan continued, "That's good, Nate. That's very good. I'm right here talking to you."

"I'm not scared," Nate protested.

"You're not scared?" Mike shouted in disbelief. "Just think about it, Nate. You've up a doggone tree."

"There's only one way down out of that tree," Dan lectured to Nate, "and you know what that is. You have to give it up, Nate. It's all garbage. You have to give it up. We were all born into this world, Nate, and we're all going to die out of it. Ain't nobody any better than anybody else. I know what you're thinking. Some people seem to be better off than others. But we're all equal human beings, Nate. The bell rings for each and every one of us. This whole thing about some people being better than other people is not real. Don't get caught up in that illusion, Nate. You have to give it up."

Mike interrupted again, this time speaking calmly to Dan, "Dan, he doesn't hear you. He doesn't hear you because he doesn't want to hear you. He's up a tree. We don't have to convince him of anything. All we have to do is know it ourselves."

Dan understood. Nevertheless, he continued his conversation with Nate, "Nate, you don't have to be up there in that tree. Do you understand what I'm saying? You need to come down. You don't have to go around trying to hurt other people in order to feel good about yourself."

"I'm not trying to hurt other people," Nate responded.

"But you *are* hurting other people, Nate. That's the problem. You are hurting other people," Dan answered.

"But I don't have any rocks. I'm not throwing rocks at anybody," Nate responded.

"No rocks, Nate. That's good. You don't have any rocks right now, but what about tomorrow or the next day? You're still up a tree, and that's what I'm trying to tell you."

"I can climb a tree if I want to."

"Nate, will you listen to me? You're missing the point. There is nothing you can do to make yourself better than other people because there's no such thing."

"But I'm not throwing rocks at people. I told you that already," Nate insisted.

Dan was so focused on Nate that he had not realized his wife was now standing next to him.

"It's time to let it go, honey," Susan said to Dan. "It's time to let it go." She took Dan's hand in hers. "Mike is right," she continued. "He's up a tree. Sometimes all we can do is know he's up a tree."

Dan looked lovingly into Susan's eyes.

"I'm sorry about this, Dan," Marvin offered.

"It's not your fault," Dan quickly answered.

"Don't take up any more of your time, and I'll stay with him," Marvin continued. "He's not gonna to be up there much longer. Now, when he comes down, I can't promise you he won't be 'up a tree' on another day. We all know how this stuff works. But I'll give him a little while longer here, and he'll come down at least for the time being."

Susan gently squeezed Dan's hand and said, "I see that you have a bruise on your right leg."

Dan looked down and noticed for the first time a bruise on the right leg just below the knee. Like many other guests at the cookout, he was wearing shorts, and the bruise was clearly visible. It was nothing major— just broken skin and minor blood to the surface.

"Let's go inside," Susan said to her husband. "I should probably put something on that." Susan and Dan walked together across the lawn toward the side entrance to the house. Those gathered at the tree began to disperse, getting back to the activities of the cookout. Only Marvin remained, waiting for his coworker to come down. About fifteen minutes later, Nate did, in fact, climb down. No one objected to Nate the person, only to his behavior. Nevertheless, Nate was feeling a bit uncomfortable after his adventure up the tree, and he left the cookout early.

At sunset, other guests started to leave. However, some moved inside and continued with conversation and other activities in the kitchen and living room of the house. Meanwhile, Dan and Cousin Charlie put away the portable canopy, the picnic table, the lawn chairs, the coolers, and the yard games.

By 10:00 p.m., all the guests were gone. Susan and Dan worked together to clean up the kitchen. Next, Dan took out the trash. Upon his return, he found Susan seated on the couch in the living room, as if she was reflecting on the day or other matters. Dan walked over and sat on the couch next to her. Susan moved over to snuggle with Dan and Dan snuggled back. At that moment, Dan felt happy and at peace. All things were not as he would like them to be, but he felt he was living a good life. He had no complaints against God. He was just thankful for all of the blessings that had come to him in his life.

Tim was a good man and he loved to work with his jackhammer, but he loved the jackhammer so much that he thought he was his jackhammer.

Myshen Nautbrae

THE ROOM SMELLED like cinnamon. There were two large candles burning on a small table nearby. We were all seated in folding chairs arranged in a circle in the spacious room in the medical-office building in an industrial complex. In the middle of our circle sat a black trunk with its lid open. I couldn't see inside, which frustrated me. The trunk was too large and deep to inspect its contents from where I was sitting. I would have had to stand up to see. And standing up just wasn't an option. Not only would it have been inappropriate (it was Tom's turn, not mine), but I also didn't want to create the impression that I was interested. I was interested, but no one needed to know that.

Tom stood up and walked to the trunk at Chris's request. He looked over the trunk for a few seconds before he pulled a garment out of it. It was a plain white T-shirt with black letters written across the chest. Tom turned it around in his hands, inspecting it.

"What do you have there, Tom?" Chris asked. Chris, a tiny woman with long red hair and one of those soothing but seemingly contrived voices, was sitting across from me in the circle holding a notebook and a clipboard. Every now and then she would look at me as if she were analyzing my movements, and I found myself expecting her to scribble something down in her notebook every time she looked over at me. She never did. I guess the notebook was just for show.

"It's the 'black man' garment," he said, holding the T-shirt up for Chris and the rest of the circle to see. The letters across the chest read: BLACK MAN.

"Well, go ahead and put it on," Chris said.

Tom obeyed.

"It's not that bad," Jasper said, crossing his arms and leaning back in his chair. "I had the 'black man' garment on one time." It was difficult to tell how old Jasper was since his face was covered in thick blond stubble, and he wore a worn red hat. But his round blue eyes gave him away. He couldn't have been much older than twenty-five.

"Are you a black man?" Chris asked. Everyone knew it was a test.

"No, I'm not a black man," Tom said.

"But you're wearing the 'black man' garment," Chris continued.

"Yeah, but I'm not a black man," he said somewhat cautiously. He ran his hand through his graying brown hair. Tom was a tall, chubby man. The white shirt tugged at his slightly protruding belly.

"Good job, Tom," Chris said, smiling and then sitting up as if rejuvenated by Tom's answer.

"I'm a white man," Tom added after a few seconds of silence. It was said as if it were an afterthought.

Chris looked literally deflated as she sank back into her chair and let out a dramatic sigh. "No, Tom," she spoke with measured patience, much in the way you would speak to a five- or six-year-old. "You're not a white man. 'White man' is an identity. It's a garment you wear just like the 'black man' garment you just put on."

"Look, I understand what you're saying. We're all the same on the inside. You learn that stuff in kindergarten. I'm not an idiot. But with all of that said and done, I'm still a white man."

Everyone stared at Chris for an answer. Tom had said what was on everyone's mind—including mine. I was more than curious about her response. It would have given me a better reason for wasting my evening in a room with a bunch of adults who were picking clothes out of a trunk and playing dress-up.

"You think you're a white man?"

"I *am* a white man," he said, the tension radiating from his eyes.

"OK," Chris said, practically throwing up her hands in surrender. "Just sit back down in your seat."

I was sorely disappointed in Chris's response to Tom's challenge. In fact, I was waiting for her answer as if some part of me depended on it. I was getting all caught up in it like I actually gave a crap about this whole thing. The truth of the matter is that I didn't care or at least I didn't at first.

Everything was fine until my enlightened husband, who has spent too much of his spare time in the last eight years reading books on personal growth and running off to workshops, decided to start diagnosing people's symptoms and making recommendations about how they could remedy any emotional or spiritual illnesses they had. It started with a few of our friends. He was passing out reading lists and suggesting programs to try out and join. I'm pretty sure that some of them didn't appreciate it. No one said anything, of course, but I know that some of them had to be ticked off because I didn't appreciate it when he found something to diagnose me with. He said that I had Myshen Nautbrae.

"What's that, Jim?" I asked him, exaggerating my exasperation. He, of course, ignored my dramatics. He pulled a couple books off the bookshelf in his office and handed them to me.

"It's when you start to believe you are what you wear," he explained with that air of confidence that his eight-year personal-growth journey had created. That attitude of his feels like a smug smile that I often want to just wipe off his face.

When Jim told me that Myshen Nautbrae was a disease, I did everything I could not to laugh because I could hear the concern in his voice. I felt perfectly fine. But my husband was concerned, so I agreed to try out therapy to "manage the illness" as my husband so gravely put it. Besides, I wanted to support my husband with his personal-growth theories. He was happier, calmer, and, for the most part, he was easier to get along with when he was theorizing. So I did it all in the interest of peace and tranquility in our marriage.

However, I do have to admit that I was a bit curious about this Myshen Nautbrae stuff and, as my husband said, I'd been "leaning a little heavy on the ego" lately. I work as a stockbroker and frankly, I was enjoying the privileges I got from my affluent lifestyle. It was easy to see the ways in which I was more successful and important than other people. These were symptoms of Myshen Nautbrae, according to Jim's definition.

"Jasper," Chris said after an awkward moment of silence, "why don't you go next?" Jasper stood up, walked to the trunk, and pulled out a garment. It was a yellow poncho. Jasper's shoulders immediately drooped, and he was frowning.

"What do you have, Jasper?" Chris asked.

"It's the 'welfare person' garment." Jasper was actually pouting.

"So what's the matter?"

"I don't want to wear it," he whined. He seemed to have regressed twenty years in age. I half expected him to stomp his feet.

"Well, somebody has to wear it. You pulled it out of the trunk." Chris went right back into the motherly tone she had used with Tom just minutes before.

"Well, I don't want to wear it," he said, mocking her. "I wore it before, and I don't like it."

"Jasper, it's nothing but the garment you wear. It's not who you are."

"I just don't see why I have to wear it all the time, and no one else does."

"Sometimes, we have to wear garments we don't like. Use it to the best of your ability. And remember, it's not who you are."

Jasper rolled his eyes and sighed before he pulled the big yellow poncho over his head. It had "WELFARE" written in black letters across the chest. He crossed his arms over the letters as if to hide the word and sat back in his seat.

There was another long moment of silence after Jasper sat down. I was sure these silent moments were meant for reflection. But instead of reflecting on Jasper and the "welfare poncho," I found myself wondering if this therapy session would let out early.

"Melissa, it's your turn to go to the trunk and take a garment," Chris said. Surprisingly, she had taken this particular moment of silence to take a few notes in her notebook. I watched Jasper watch Chris take down notes. I imagined that if we were being graded, she would have been writing a D or F beside Jasper's name.

"I'd rather not, if you don't mind," Melissa said. She was a thin woman with light brown skin. She had her thick dark hair tied in a bun.

"You'd rather not? I don't understand."

"There's nothing wrong with me."

I was glad to hear her say that. I certainly felt the same way. I was in a room with a bunch of losers, and I didn't belong. These people just didn't know how to accept who they were and be proud of themselves and their accomplishments. Or perhaps they lacked any real accomplishments. That was probably their problem, not Myshen Nautbrae.

"You're suffering from Myshen Nautbrae," Chris told her. "It's nothing to be ashamed of."

"We all have it," Tom added.

I had to hold back a snicker.

"Well, there's nothing wrong with me. A friend recommended this to me, but I can see now that it was mistake for me to come here."

"It's certainly up to you. Nobody is going to force you do anything that you don't want to do."

"I'm a banker, and my ancestors were Greek. I'm proud of that. That's who I am."

"You feel good about that, Melissa?" Jasper asked.

"Yes, I do," she said looking over at Jasper in his "welfare poncho."

"But that's not who you are," Jasper answered.

A look of annoyance and confusion washed over Melissa's face. She looked as if she were consciously holding back a thought. "This is not for me," she said.

"Then, I would respectfully ask that you leave the room. It would be disruptive for you to sit here and not participate," Chris said.

"I understand," she said. We sat in stiff silence as we listened to Melissa leave the room—the sound of her rising from her seat and stepping out of the circle, the sound of her shoes on the floor as she made her way to the door, and the sound of the door as it opened and closed behind her with a muffled bang then click. It was unsettling, to say the least. I was pleased that Melissa spoke up about being proud of her identity, but I never expected her to get kicked out.

"Let's take a moment to settle down," Chris said to the group, obviously picking up on the tension that Melissa's exit had caused. "As we sit in our garments, whatever they may be, fully aware of what they are, let's see if we can sense the self that lies quietly within, beneath it all." I stared at Melissa's empty chair.

It was nearly five minutes before Chris resumed the session. It was my turn. I reached into the trunk and felt around and pulled out a garment. It was a navy-blue jacket to a man's suit. I looked it over. There was a label pinned on the front pocket of the jacket. I stared at it a moment and then thought, *How cool is that?*

"What do you have, Joan?" Chris asked me.

"It's the stockbroker garment."

"Then, go ahead and put it on," she told me. I did. It was entirely too big. I felt like a little kid who just put on her father's jacket. My fingertips were barely peeking out of the sleeves.

"Are you a stockbroker?" Chris asked. I smiled. The irony was too incredible.

"Well, yes, as a matter of fact, I am," I answered.

"Stockbroker—that's just a garment you pulled out of the trunk," Chris said.

"Well, no. You're not going to believe this, but I really am a stockbroker."

"That's not who you are, Joan. It's just the garment you wear," Jasper added. I felt a twinge of annoyance. I wasn't about to be lectured by man in a big yellow poncho with "WELFARE" written across the chest.

"No, I don't think you understand what I'm saying to you. I really am a stockbroker. In real life, I'm a stockbroker."

"OK, thanks, Joan. Why don't you just return to your seat?" Chris said. I wanted to say something to make them appreciate the strange

ROGER L. BREWER AND NICOLE BREWER

coincidence, but no one seemed interested in my true occupation. I sat down more than a little disturbed. But not only was I disturbed I felt belittled. And I wasn't about to be belittled by these people.

"Do you say I have Myshen Nautbrae because I believe I'm a stock-broker, which by the way, is precisely what I am?" I tried to mask my irritation. I did so poorly.

"The short answer to that question is yes," Chris said.

"Yes?"

"Yes," she said.

"Well, if I have Myshen Nautbrae because I believe I'm stockbroker, which I am, then most people in our society must have the same condition. Because for sure, the bankers, plumbers, doctors, and whatnots believe they are the bankers, plumbers, doctors, and whatnots."

"Joan," Chris said calmly, "the ills of our society are the ills of our society. I'm just as troubled as you are. But right now at this particular moment, in this particular place, my concern is with you."

I'm sure it is of no surprise that I didn't return to therapy. My husband, of course, was disappointed, but he'll get over it. He'll have to get over it because I'm obviously not going back. I'll continue to support him within reason in his personal-growth adventures. They're important to him, so, on some level, they are important to me. It's just that the Myshen Nautbrae escapade was a bit too much for me to handle. As Melissa said, that stuff just isn't for me.

If you're already at home sitting in front of the fireplace, don't argue with the drunk who says you can't get there.

CARL IS NOT STUPID

MRS. BRITMORE IS a true professional. She takes great pride in teaching her third-grade class. Clearly, she is making a difference in the lives of her young students.

The students, as usual, settled into their seats to begin the day. And, as usual, Mrs. Britmore stood in front of the class with a presence that demanded her students' undivided attention.

"Good morning, everyone," her voice resounded.

"Good morning, Mrs. Britmore," was the reply.

"Does anybody know what today is?" she asked. "It's a special day in our school district, especially over at the high school. One day, you'll be in high school, too."

"My brother is in high school, and he's taking a science test today," a student replied.

"Yes, a science test is special, very special, and very important, too. But I'm thinking of something a little different," Mrs. Britmore said.

Becky, seated up front, raised her hand and was recognized by Mrs. Britmore.

"It's Carl Is Not Stupid Day," she said.

"Yes, it's Carl Is Not Stupid Day. Very good, Becky."

Becky smiled proudly. But it was no surprise to anyone that she would have the correct answer.

"What's so important about Carl Is Not Stupid Day?" Mrs. Britmore asked.

Becky immediately raised her hand again. But Mrs. Britmore wanted to get other students involved and looked away from Becky, waiting for other responses.

A student across the room raised her hand and was acknowledged by Mrs. Britmore. "It means Carl is not stupid. Carl is just like everybody else," the student said.

Another student responded, "Some people think Carl is stupid. And that's why we have this day."

"Thank you for those good answers," Mrs. Britmore replied. "People who think Carl is stupid are wrong. And we have this special day to remind them that Carl is not stupid. He's the same as everybody else."

Mrs. Britmore paused for a moment to allow silence to fill the room. She wanted to give her students an opportunity to reflect on what she had just said before continuing.

"What else can you tell me about Carl? Who is Carl? Where did he come from? And why do some people think he's stupid?"

Becky was anxious to get back into the conversation. This time she did not raise her hand. "Carl is a junior in high school. And he grew up in this town and went through our schools just like everybody else," she said.

"And what else?" Mrs. Britmore interjected, again trying to get others involved.

"But I'm not finished, Mrs. Britmore," Becky insisted.

"What else would you like to say, Becky?"

"I want to start at the beginning."

"OK, if you wish."

"Well, in the beginning, Carl's parents came to our town to work in the orchards."

"Very good."

"Then Carl was born. But when he started going to school, everybody thought he was stupid."

"And why did they think he was stupid?"

"Because he was poor and didn't wear nice clothes, and because his parents worked in the orchards."

"That's excellent, Becky. Thank you. Now, let's give someone else a chance. What was it like for Carl as he was going to school?"

"The kids would make fun of him and wouldn't play with him," a student answered.

Another student added, "The teachers weren't fair to him either. Everybody thought he was stupid."

"Well, not everybody," Mrs. Britmore said. "But anyway," she continued, "it was a very sad period in our history, for our school district, and for our town. Fortunately, we have now moved beyond that. Today, Carl is treated with the same dignity and respect as everybody else. And we're doing all we can to correct the horrible mistakes of our past."

A student raised his hand and without waiting to be recognized asked, "Mrs. Britmore, when did Carl stop being stupid?"

"Carl was never stupid in the first place," Mrs. Britmore responded. "That's one of the most important messages we can learn from Carl Is Not Stupid Day. Carl was never stupid, but unfortunately it took people a long time to understand that. As a school district, we didn't know he wasn't stupid until he was in the seventh grade."

"Wow!" the student exclaimed.

Mrs. Britmore picked a file up from the top of her desk and then turned back to face the class.

"To help us understand that Carl is the same as everybody else," Mrs. Britmore resumed, "let's talk about some of his achievements."

A student seated near the center of the classroom, raised his hand.

"Yes, Milo," Mrs. Britmore said.

"He played soccer in the fourth grade," Milo answered.

"Good," Mrs. Britmore said.

"He was in the Boy Scouts, and he joined the library club," another student said.

"That's good, very good. Thank you. Let me hear a few things now about how he did with his school work."

Becky raised her hand.

"Yes, Becky," Mrs. Britmore said.

"I think he got an A in math in the sixth grade."

"Yes," Mrs. Britmore said, looking at the papers in her hands. "An A in math and also an A in Spanish."

"What's that you're reading, Mrs. Britmore?" Milo asked.

"This is a copy of Carl's academic record," Mrs. Britmore explained. "And it shows that Carl has had good academic success."

"But he didn't get all As," Becky interjected.

"Well, nobody gets all As," Mrs. Britmore responded. Becky immediately raised her hand again. "Well, most people don't get all As," Mrs. Britmore added.

Mrs. Britmore noticed that two boys over in the corner near the window were engaged in a bit of side chatter. This was unacceptable. However, she did not want to stifle or intimidate her pupils. She wanted to be considerate but firm. She walked over to their desks.

"Is there a question you boys have in mind or perhaps there's something you would like to add to our discussion? I apologize if I did not recognize you earlier."

"I was wondering if Carl ever got any bad grades," a small boy with dark-rimmed glasses said. "Did he ever get any Fs on his report card?"

"Many students, at one time or another, have problems with certain classes," Mrs. Britmore explained.

"Carl did well in his classes, but not as well as other students. And that's because of the way he was treated," Becky added.

"I was about to make that point. Thank you, Becky," Mrs. Britmore commented as she walked back to the front of the class. "Carl was treated badly in our schools, and that affected his performance. But he was still able to do well, although not as well as other students."

As the discussion continued, Mrs. Britmore felt tremendous pride in her students for their sensitivity to Carl and their knowledge of his history, and most importantly for their understanding that he was not stupid. She was confident that her students would grow up to become outstanding citizens in their communities.

Meanwhile, it was a great day at the high school. A huge "Carl Is Not Stupid" banner hung on the wall near the front entrance of the building. Other similar but smaller banners were hung in classrooms and at other locations throughout the school. In the different classrooms, teachers discussed Carl's achievements and promoted the important message that "Carl Is Not Stupid." The final ceremony was an afternoon school assembly during which the principal personally congratulated Carl and spoke to the entire school student body on the importance of the day.

Carl couldn't have been happier as he sat in the auditorium listening to the praise that the principal offered. It had been a long time coming, but Carl was starting to feel truly appreciated. Along with his teachers and many of his fellow classmates, Carl was proud that he was finally being recognized as not stupid. And because of it all, it certainly felt like a close to perfect day for Carl and the town in which he lived.

And the dog awakened from a restful night's sleep. The cat had hated him all night long, and he didn't feel anything at all.

WHAT'S THE MATTER WITH CHARLIE FRANK JOHNSON?

Jack Minifield was a tall, dark man with big, round eyes. He used to be a sharecropper, but he stopped doing that and got a job down at the "chicken shack" plant. Him and his wife named Essie Mae lived in a house down that dirt road what you see just before you get to Sawmill Junction. They had two boys and three girls, all of 'em still going to school and everything.

When the car drove up in the yard, the youngest girl named Mary Ann ran in the house to get her daddy. By the time Jack got out on the front porch, the preacher, a thin-looking older man, was already out of his car. Jack walked out in the yard and met him and shook his hand.

"I appreciate you coming out here like you said you would, Reverend Dawson."

"I figure it's the least I can do. Getting me to come out here is the one reason you came to church this morning. We ought to be real plain about that up front," the preacher said.

Jack was just a little embarrassed. "From now on," he promised, "I'm gonna start coming to church like I'm supposed to."

"We'll see about that. So where's the boy right now, Jack? Is he around here somewhere?"

"He's in the house sitting on the sofa."

The little girl named Mary Ann was standing there listening. She ran into the house to get Charlie Frank.

"Exactly what do you want me to do with the boy?" the preacher asked.

"Like I told you, I want you to see if you can fix him."

"People ain't like cars, Jack, where you can take a screwdriver or something and just make 'em do what you want."

"I know what you mean by that, Reverend. But the boy can't go on acting the way he's acting."

Charlie Frank Johnson came out of the house and onto the front porch. Mary Ann was right behind him. Charlie Frank was a twenty-four-year-old man, tall and dark like Jack, but he didn't have big eyes.

"Uncle Jack, you wanna talk to me?" Charlie Frank asked.

Jack waved his hand for Charlie Frank to come on out in the yard where he and the preacher were standing. Charlie Frank walked out there.

"This here is Reverend Dawson," Jack said. "He came out here so you and him can have a talk. I figured that would be all right with you."

Charlie Frank nodded.

"Then go ahead and get in the car," the preacher said. "We'll take a ride somewhere."

Charlie Frank got in the car like the preacher said.

"You're a good man, Reverend Dawson," Jack said to the preacher. "If you can't say something to get the boy turned around, then I figure there ain't nothing nobody can do for him."

"Just wait a minute with all that stuff," the preacher answered. "Let me talk to the boy, and we'll see what happens."

Then the preacher got in his car and crunk it up. He backed out the yard and drove off up the road with Charlie Frank in the car with him.

Now Charlie Frank Johnson came from Alabama. It was Alabama where he got into trouble when he hit a man upside the head with a Coca-Cola bottle. The man had it coming, but Charlie Frank still had no business hitting him in the head like that. The man was hurt so bad that everybody thought he was gonna die, and Charlie Frank had to go to prison for what he did. When he got out of prison his mamma told him he needed to go somewhere and get a new start. So he went across the state line to live with his Uncle Jack just long enough to get on his own two feet.

The first thing Charlie Frank did when he got to his Uncle Jack's house was to go out looking for job. He ended up working with four other fellas cutting down pulpwood and hauling it off. That pulpwood job wasn't supposed to last but two or three months or something like that. But that didn't bother Charlie Frank none because at least he was working.

Everything was going all right so far. Then one evening around seven o'clock, Jack went to the store to buy some bread and some meat. When he came back out the store to get in his car, this fella named Ned came up and started talking to him. Ned was one of them same pulpwood fellas what was working with Charlie Frank. Jack knowed Ned for a long time—used to go hunting with his older brother.

Ned looked Jack straight in the eye and told him, "Your nephew Charlie Frank is a good worker, but he goes off somewhere from time to time and stands there by himself. Looks like he be praying." No sooner than Jack heard that, he knowed exactly what Ned was talking about. Him and the children had seen Charlie Frank acting the same way around the house. Every now and then, and nobody knowed what for, Charlie Frank would just go off somewhere and be by himself. When you'd look around, he might be at the woodpile or under a tree. Ain't no telling; he might be leaning up against the chicken house or somewhere else like that. Sometimes he'd be standing up, and sometimes he'd be sitting down, one or the other. Anyhow, he would shut his eyes and put his hands together and everything; it sure did look like he'd be praying.

But Jack, being the kinda fella he was, never said anything to Charlie Frank about the way he was acting. Jack figured that as long as Charlie Frank wasn't bothering anybody, what he did around the house was his own business. Of course, what you do around the house you can't always do when you're out somewhere else, and Jack knowed that. He kinda thought Charlie Frank knowed it, too.

"It don't bother me to see a fella praying," Ned said. "It's just a little strange to see a fella praying on the job like that. We be cutting pulpwood."

When Jack got back home from the store that night, he was thinking real hard about what Ned had told him. Not that he had changed his mind or anything because he still felt that what Charlie Frank was doing was Charlie Frank's business. But now that other folks had started talking about it and everything, Jack thought that maybe he should at least speak to his nephew just to find out what was going on. But by the time he made up his mind to go ahead and do it, Charlie Frank was already sprawled out on the sofa and had gone to sleep for the rest of the night.

Jack came home from work the next day like he always did. When it got close to time for Charlie Frank to get off from work, he went out and sat down on the front porch to wait for his nephew to get home. In a little while, that pulpwood truck drove up and dropped Charlie Frank off. Jack just walked out in the front yard and met him, and they both walked over and sat down at the woodpile.

"I'm gonna come right to the point," Jack said. "Every now and then you be standing around praying on the job. That's what I heard."

Charlie Frank didn't say anything at first because he was thinking about what his Uncle Jack had just said.

"You be praying on the job," Jack repeated. "You go off by yourself, put your hands together, and you be praying on the job."

"I don't be praying on the job," Charlie Frank said.

"Me and the children seen you doing it around the house."

"I don't be praying," Charlie Frank said. "I wouldn't lie to you about that, Uncle Jack, with you letting me stay here with you and everything. I don't be praying when you see me doing something every now and then. What I be doing is hating people."

Now Jack never expected something like that to come out of Charlie Frank's mouth. And he knowed he heard him right; at least he thought he did.

"What do you mean by you be hating people?" Jack asked his nephew, just to be sure he understood.

"I just be hating 'em."

"But how do you do that, Charlie Frank?"

"It ain't hard."

"I know it ain't hard, boy. That ain't what I said. I said how you be doing it."

"I just think about it, that's all."

"You think about what?"

"I think about hating 'em."

Jack shook his head like he couldn't believe it. "Your mamma know you be hating people?"

"She's been hollering at me about it."

Jack hadn't ever seen or heard tale of anybody hating people like what his nephew was doing. He was so shaken up about what Charlie Frank told him that he had to get up on his feet and look the other way. Charlie Frank just kept sitting there. He knowed his Uncle wasn't through with him.

Jack turned back around and asked Charlie Frank. "When you be hating people, do you be talking to yourself about that or what?"

"I be talking to myself."

"Well, that's what I wanna know."

"Sometimes I just be thinking."

"What do you be thinking, boy?"

"I be thinking I hate 'em."

"And who do you hate, Charlie Frank? Can you tell me that?"

"Yes, sir."

"Well, go ahead and tell me."

Charlie Frank thought about it a little bit before he started talking. "I hate them people what got the pretty clothes and the pretty houses," he said. "They think they're better than me. They look at you the wrong way, and they be saying stuff what don't make you feel good."

Then Charlie Frank shut his eyes and put his hands together and kept on talking. "I hate that Miss Hudson woman. She's the schoolteacher what got the pretty hair. She don't like it if you're poor. She called me stupid in fifth grade 'cause I couldn't say my lesson. I hate that Wilson boy, the one what used to pick on me all the time. He didn't think I was worth nothing. He was bigger than me, and we done both growed up now, but I still hate him. I don't like them people, them ones what be putting you down all the time."

Charlie Frank stopped for a little bit to swallow and take a breath. Then he went back to talking. "I hate my daddy, too, 'cause my daddy used to beat me when I hadn't done nothing. One time I saw my daddy hit my mamma with his fist. I don't hate my daddy too bad, but I still hate him."

"Charlie Frank," Jack interrupted. "I want you to open up your eyes."

"Yes, sir," Charlie Frank said. He opened his eyes.

Charlie Frank wanted to go on naming the people he hated. But Jack, being scared of God and everything, got a little nervous. He didn't like seeing Charlie Frank looking like he was praying, but at the same time just hating people.

"You think you getting something out of it when you go around hating people like that?" Jack asked his nephew.

Charlie Frank wasn't quite sure what his Uncle was asking, but he answered anyway.

"You mean, how come I hate people? I hate people 'cause they done something to me."

"But how come you hate 'em? Do it make you feel good?"

"It don't make me feel good."

"Then how come you hate 'em?"

"I hate 'em, Uncle Jack, 'cause that's what I'm supposed to do. If somebody done something to you, you suppose to hate 'em."

Jack started thinking right then and there about what to do about his nephew. He wasn't gonna put him out of the house or anything like that because Charlie Frank was his sister's boy, his oldest sister's boy. They were kinsfolk, and kinsfolk just don't quit on kinsfolk. But he sure didn't like the way Charlie Frank was thinking.

"Uncle Jack," Charlie Frank went on, "what's wrong with hating people if they done something wrong to you? That's what I always be asking my mamma."

"Well, it just ain't right, Charlie Frank. That's all I can tell you."

"But you can't let people go around messing with you."

"I ain't saying you have to let people mess with you."

"If somebody mess with me, I'm gonna fight 'em."

Jack kept on talking to Charlie Frank and arguing with him and everything, and when he got through he went straight in the house and into the kitchen where Essie Mae was cooking supper. He started telling Essie Mae everything what was going on, and that's when Essie Mae said, "Maybe the preacher can talk some sense into the boy." Jack thought about what Essie Mae said, but it didn't take long. He know'd Essie Mae was right.

It was dark outside by the time the preacher brought Charlie Frank back home. Jack had been walking around doing this and that while they were gone, but when the car rolled up in the yard, he was sitting on the front porch with the front porch light on. Charlie Frank got out the car, walked up on the porch, and kept on into the house. Jack looked at him when he walked by to see if he had a different kind of look on his face or something like that, but he couldn't see no difference.

The preacher was still sitting in the car, and Jack walked out there to talk to him.

"Me and the boy had a good talk," the preacher said.

"I hope that means he's gonna stop hating people."

"I can't say that. Actually, the boy is pretty much set in his ways."

"So, what's gonna happen to him?"

84

"I don't know what's gonna happen to him."

"I mean, is he gonna go to hell or something like that?" Jack asked, now getting a little mad at the preacher.

"He might. But that ain't for me to say." The preacher said in his normal voice; he didn't seem to be upset with anybody.

"I just don't want to see him keep hating people like he doing."

"You know what, Jack? When you think about it, he ain't much different from the rest of us, if you know what I mean."

"I don't think I do know what you mean, Reverend Dawson."

"You hold grudges against people, don't you, Jack? I bet you can name a few people you'd like to get even with."

"But I don't go around like I'm praying about it."

"Well, thank God for that."

Having spoken his mind, the preacher didn't have anything else to say, and he started backing up his car to leave. "I'll see you in church come next Sunday," he told Jack, and then he drove off up the road. Jack just stood there for a little bit, not quite sure what to think about anything.

The next day Jack was still kinda mad at the preacher. He didn't like it when the preacher said he wasn't no better than Charlie Frank. He fretted about the whole thing for a day or two before he got over it.

Not long after that, Charlie Frank left that pulpwood job and started working for a man helping him out doing construction work. Then he found his own place to live and moved out of his Uncle's house.

Charlie Frank Johnson kept on living his life the way he thought he should. He never stopped hating people for as long as he could breathe. And being the kind of fella he was, he never thought for even one second that he was ever any worse off for it.

PART 2

Why You Need a Strategy
to Protect Yourself

————— ⌒ —————

WHAT'S THE MOST effective way to respond to someone who commits an act of bigotry against you? Obviously it depends on the circumstances. If someone assaults you physically or otherwise denies you your rights or privileges, you may take action to hold the individual accountable. You may seek remedies or compensation for injuries or damages sustained. If the bigotry against you does not involve a physical assault or the denial of material rights or privileges, you may choose to confront the individual responsible or otherwise stand up for yourself. But what do you do to protect yourself from the loss of self-esteem and other mental and emotional harm you suffer when bigotry is committed against you?

What if you could make it so that no one could hurt you on the inside by committing bigotry, discrimination, bullying, or other disrespect against you? What if someone could say something or do something to try to put you down, but you would not feel hurt on the inside or diminished in any way in how you feel about yourself? Of course, you would still have to hold the bigot accountable, seek remedies to which you are entitled, and stand up for yourself in other ways available for you to do so. But what if you could prevent getting hurt on the inside?

Certainly, if people would only stop committing bigotry and other disrespect against their fellow human beings, there would be no bigotry and therefore no mental and emotional harm caused by it. So why not go right to cause of the mental and emotional harm, eliminate bigotry and other disrespect altogether, and be done with the problem? Why not, indeed! The reality is, however, that society will not or cannot make all things right, at least not at the moment. Just think about it. When will that day come when everyone in society is treated with dignity and respect: within twenty years…fifty years…one hundred years? Within the next two centuries? Will it *ever* happen?

It makes absolutely no sense to leave yourself vulnerable on the inside as the bigot continues to commit bigotry and other disrespect against you. Protecting yourself on the inside and eliminating all bigotry and prejudice are not mutually exclusive objectives. Actually, they go hand in hand. You can and must pursue both at the same time. Therefore, you must never stop the work you are doing to abolish harmful behavior altogether. To stop your fight against bigotry and other disrespect would be ridiculous. All of society must continue its work to end bigotry. But at the same time, it is essential that individuals protect themselves from mental and emotional harm.

The act of bigotry is much like a snakebite. Both occurrences have two very definite components: the bite/act itself *and* the insertion of poison into the individual. The venom from the snakebite damages the physical body. The venom from bigotry penetrates the mind and emotions and causes loss of self-esteem and other mental and emotional harm. If someone who has been bitten by a poisonous snake were to come to you for advice about treatment, would you recommend that he or she do nothing about the poison penetrating within and work *only* to eliminate all snakebites in the world? Obviously, that advice would not be wise. So why would you work *only* to eliminate bigotry and other disrespect and not take action to protect yourself in the meantime from the mental and emotional harm you suffer on the inside?

You can learn much about how bigotry harms you on the inside by simply identifying the different negative thoughts and feelings you experience when someone does something or says something to try to put you down. When someone puts you down, how does it make you feel? Do you feel unimportant? Do you feel disrespected? Do you feel defeated, discouraged, or disappointed? Do you feel anger, resentment, hatred, or fear? Do you question or doubt your sense of self-worth? Of course, you not may experience all of these negative thoughts and feelings every time someone puts you down. Nevertheless, if you feel one or more on each occasion, there is a negative impact on the quality of your life.

Don't be deceived by the misguided notion that you are already fully protected by existing laws and regulations. While it is true that state and federal laws have greatly reduced discriminatory practices in the United States, far too many people do not always honor or respect these laws, and discrimination continues. In addition, most of the mental and emotional harm people suffer today does not result from the violation of laws or regulations. Mental and emotional harm in the United States today is predominantly caused by insults, implications, suggestions, disparaging comments, bigoted attitudes, innuendos, and other subtle (but very significant) behaviors that do not violate any laws. It is naive to think bigoted behavior is harmful only if it breaks the law. Much of the mental and emotional harm people suffer today is beyond the reach of legislation.

Also, some people may argue that although discrimination exists, no one in the United States today actually experiences bigotry on a daily basis. Therefore, some may ask how could anyone be truly harmed on the inside in a significant way if he or she experiences bigotry only every once and a while. It is true that some people who experience an act bigotry today may not encounter another act of bigotry for a month or two later or even longer. But even if you experience the act of bigotry itself only every once and a while, the memory of that incident and the pain associated with that memory continues well beyond the day on which the bigotry occurs. In addition, you are likely to have continuous fear and anxiety about when the next act will be committed against you.

Mental and emotional harm caused by bigotry stays with you in your memory of what happened in the past *and* in your fear and anticipation of what will happen in the future. Moreover, if society holds prejudice against you, intimidation and other mental and emotional harm will be felt by you even when no specific acts of bigotry (past, present, or future) are committed against you. Your knowledge alone that people have prejudice against you adversely affects your mental and emotional well-being.

Mental and emotional harm caused by bigotry and other disrespect is huge. Don't be misled by statements to the contrary. It is unpleasant, discomforting, painful, disturbing, and continuous. It negatively affects how you feel inside, how you feel about yourself, how you feel about others, and how you feel about the world in which you live. It impairs you in your ability to live the quality of life that you deserve. There is no way that you can have the high level of inner peace and happiness you deserve if mental and emotional pain caused by others is a big part of your life experience.

So why would you *not* do something now to take away the mental and emotional pain you suffer? After all, do you not go to a doctor or take pain medication when you have significant physical pain or discomfort? Why would you not do likewise and take action to relieve your mental and emotional pain? For sure, mental and emotional pain is not the same as physical pain, but it is just as real, bringing to bear great discomfort and "dis-ease" in your everyday life.

In addition to the mental and emotional harm described so far, you also suffer loss of self-esteem when others put you down. The loss of self-esteem is also painful. How can you not have pain on the inside if you feel inferior as a human being? But the loss of self-esteem penetrates further and directly impairs you in your ability to achieve in society at the same level as others.

Whenever you encounter an act of bigotry or other disrespect, of whatever kind, the perpetrator is saying (directly or indirectly) that you are inferior as a human being. If you hear this statement repeatedly in your life and do nothing to protect yourself on the inside, it negatively affects how you feel about yourself and your place in society.

Some people may argue that scientific study does not establish without a doubt that bigotry and other disrespect actually cause the loss of self-esteem. But you do not need scientific study or expert testimony to know the truth. You know the truth based on your life experience and observation and understanding of human behavior. It's all a matter of common sense. If others continue repeatedly to declare you unworthy, and you do nothing to protect yourself, you are likely to believe or give credit to what they are saying about you.

By the way, self-esteem is not the same as having confidence in a particular skill or ability. For example, your belief that you can perform well in music, sports, math, science, politics, business, or other areas is not self-esteem. Confidence in a skill or ability may help to build your self-esteem, but it does not *necessarily* have that effect. Self-esteem is not about what you can do but how you feel about yourself as a human being. Do you feel you are a valuable human being, just as valuable as anyone and everyone else in the world, *or* do you feel inferior and not worth much of anything at all? Most people probably fall somewhere between the high and the low ends of this spectrum.

How does low self-esteem adversely affect your ability to achieve or accomplish things in life at the same level as others? Actually, the answer is quite simple. If you want to accomplish something in life, you have to try. You have to make the effort. If you don't try, you're going nowhere. If you want to become a carpenter, a teacher, an electrician, or whatever else you may aspire to, you have to try. If you want to go to school and do well there, you have to try. If you don't try, the ball game's over. If you don't try, you have taken yourself out of the game altogether.

Of course, there are various reasons why people do not try to accomplish important things in life. Some don't want to do the work that is required. Some are not willing to make necessary sacrifices. Some feel they don't have the ability. But many who are otherwise very capable and have the ability to succeed do not even try because of low self-esteem. They feel diminished on the inside and do not have a sufficient sense of self-worth to make the effort necessary to achieve.

Also, people with low self-esteem who *do* try to accomplish different goals are still at a great disadvantage. When you do try to accomplish things in life, you almost always encounter obstacles and challenges along the way. For example, sometimes there are a limited number of opportunities available to do what you want to do. Sometimes specific people or things work against you. Sometimes you don't have the money or the connections. Sometimes other obligations or responsibilities hold you back. And sometimes things just don't go your way.

Some people are able to move through the challenges and obstacles they encounter because they try harder than others. They don't give up. But if you have low self-esteem, you are less likely to try as hard as others. If you don't feel good about yourself as a human being, you are more likely than not to give up at the first sign of trouble or at least not make your best effort. On the other hand, if you feel good about yourself as a human being, you are more likely to continue to try despite the difficulties you face. And when you continue to try with your best effort, you are more likely than not to accomplish the things in your life you wish to accomplish.

Your failure to try, or your failure to try hard enough due to low self-esteem caused by bigotry and other disrespect, is essentially a denial of equal opportunity to achieve in life. State and federal civil-rights laws in the United States are designed to provide equal opportunity for all. As a matter of reality, however, unless you have good self-esteem, equal opportunity does not exist. State and federal civil-rights laws are vital, but they have their limitations. If you suffer bigotry and prejudice, you will never have equal opportunity until you take control over how you feel about yourself as a human being.

Furthermore, if you have low self-esteem, you are less likely than otherwise to reach out into the wider world (at work, at school, or wherever you may find yourself) to build and maintain good relationships with others. Good relationships have value not only because they nourish you on the inside but also because they are connections. When you interact with others in a meaningful and positive way, you establish a valuable network of people, and some in your network may be able to assist you with one or more of your life ambitions.

Some in your network may end up providing you with financial assistance, hiring you for a job, offering you a business opportunity, or otherwise providing you directly with a material benefit. Others in your network, who know and respect you, will tell you about opportunities that interest you. They will put you in contact with people who can help you. They will suggest or recommend you for jobs and other advancements. They will encourage you, provide you with important information, and give you ideas to help you along the way.

Many people who achieve at a high level in our society today do so because they get valuable support and assistance from friends, family, and others in their network. As a result, people no better qualified than you, or perhaps even less qualified than you, get education, training, jobs, promotions, business opportunities, and other advancements "ahead of you" because of their connections. If there is no one in your network to provide you with similar support, you are at a great disadvantage.

When you have good relationships with others in a network of people who know and respect you, you are much more likely than not to achieve the things in life that are important to you. To build and maintain a valuable network, you have to feel good about yourself as a human being. If you don't feel good about yourself, you will probably associate only with those people with whom you are comfortable. You are not likely to put yourself out there in the wider world where other important contacts and relationships can be established. As a result, you do not get the benefit of networking that others enjoy, and ultimately you suffer in your ability to achieve at the same level as others. Don't let anybody fool you. Networking is huge in acquiring jobs and other opportunities in any society.

Mental and emotional harm caused by bigotry and other disrespect is not an immediate life-or-death situation. If you do nothing to protect yourself from this harm, it is unlikely that you will suddenly keel over and die as a result. But the harm you suffer is still the harm you suffer. It diminishes the quality of your life and denies you equal opportunity to succeed. Is there any good reason to suffer this harm when it is within your power to take it out of your life?

Some who do not understand or care about mental and emotional harm caused by bigotry may argue, "What's the big deal? Get over it. Everybody must deal with adversity." Your answer to this point of view is that you *will* get over it, no thanks to the bigot. However, you will get over it only after you take action on your own to protect yourself on the inside. Unfortunately, some people will never understand that those of us who belong to certain groups in society are reminded daily, in subtle and not so subtle ways, that society deems us as inferior. We are confronted with this negative attitude day after day after day as we interact with others and encounter information from television, newspapers, the Internet, and other media.

Bigotry, if you've experienced it in your life, is like a little bird fixed on one of your shoulders, telling you at different times during each day, "You know what, John? You're inferior." Each individual occurrence of this negative chatter of the bird on your shoulder—if it happens only two or three times a day or even less—may seem insignificant, but the continuation of this chatter over and over again, day after day, is devastating.

Bigotry in small doses can very deceptive. When you experience bigotry in this way, you may not even appreciate that something harmful is happening to you. Your negative encounters become your "new normal." It does not occur to you that things can or should be different. If you do recognize there is harm, you perceive that harm as inconsequential and just take the hit. You are not inclined to protect yourself on the inside. The truth of the matter is that over a period of time, after you have repeatedly experienced one dose of bigotry after another, considerable mental and emotional harm will have occurred.

If you experience prejudice, discrimination, bigotry, bullying, or other disrespect in your life, whether based on race, religion, gender, nationality, sexual orientation, skin color, language, age, economic status, occupation, physical appearance, physical ability, or whatever the case may be, you need to implement a specific strategy into your life to protect yourself on the inside. The little bird on your shoulder is telling you, probably each and every day, that you're inferior. On some days you hear it multiple times. At the moment, you may not be able to stop the devious chatter of this bird altogether, but for sure you can change what you hear the bird saying.

Introduction to the Strategy

The specific plan or method that we recommend to protect yourself from mental and emotional harm caused by bigotry and other disrespect has five different components: (1) recognize all bigotry as a lie, (2) awaken to the bigot's motivation, (3) detach from your roles and identities, (4) don't debate the lie, and (5) abandon all hostilities that you may be harboring against those who perpetrate wrongs against you. In this book we provide you with sufficient information to understand these components and implement them into your life.

Origin of the Different Components

You may have noticed already, for example, in our accounts of our respective youths, that the different components of this strategy did not originate with us, the authors of this book. Actually, the components have been around for a very long time. Indeed, you may recognize one or more as something you or someone you know use already. But people who may already be using one or more of these components are probably not using all of them, or they're not using all of them with the consistency necessary to make a significant difference in their lives.

What we have to offer is that we have identified the different techniques, practices, and understandings that you need to protect yourself, and we have put them together in a single strategy. We recommend that you use this strategy intentionally as a shield. To get the results you need, you must use the complete strategy on a consistent basis and with the specific purpose of protecting yourself on the inside.

The strategy we recommend is a very powerful instrument that will produce some results immediately after you begin using it. However, it takes time and effort to make the strategy fully come alive for yourself. Your progress will depend on your individual effort and ability to implement the concepts and understandings into your life. You may never reach the point where you are totally and completely free from *all* mental and emotional harm. But if you make the effort and spend the necessary time, you will greatly diminish the loss of self-esteem and other mental and emotional harm you otherwise would suffer. Even though you may not reach the mountaintop, your personal growth alone will lift your burden enormously and greatly improve the overall quality of your life.

How You Know the Strategy Works

You do not need scientific study or expert testimony to know the strategy works. All you need is common sense. When you recognize all bigotry as a lie, you know as a matter of logic and common sense that you diminish or eliminate the mental and emotional impact of bigotry. When you understand the bigot operates out of fear and weakness, you know that you take away much of the bigot's mental and emotional power over you. When you are mindful that your sense of self-worth comes from within, you know that you are strengthened and empowered on the inside. When you no longer feel compelled to prove your self-worth, you know that you relieve yourself of a heavy burden. When you are no longer encumbered by feelings of hatred, anger or resentment, you know that the quality of your life improves.

In addition, we also offer our personal testimonies as stated in the introduction to this book. The strategy worked for us, and it will work for you as well. We are not saying that you will obtain everything in life that you desire. What we are saying is that when you protect yourself on the inside, you put yourself in the best possible position to achieve at a high level and feel good about yourself despite the bigotry, prejudice, or other disrespect you encounter in your life. And this benefit is enormous.

Self-Esteem Not Based on Achievement

It is important for you to know the strategy we recommend does not advocate building self-esteem based on material achievement. Achievement is an essential part of the human experience; there is no question about that. Achievement at a high level, such as graduating from college, getting a promotion, or winning an award for excellence, can make you feel very proud of yourself. We are not being critical of achievement. But when you rely on achievement for self-esteem, your strong sense of self-worth is uncertain and often a long time coming, if at all. Truly, you should not have to live with uncertainty or wait an indefinite period of time to feel good about yourself.

Furthermore, in many cases, achieving at a level that makes you feel good about yourself may first require good self-esteem in order for you to achieve at that high level, which is paradoxical. Relying on achievement is a trap. It is much like the quandary of being denied a job because you don't have the necessary experience but being unable to get the necessary experience until you actually get the job. In addition, even if you are fortunate enough to achieve at a high level, achievement *alone* does not necessarily improve self-esteem or eliminate mental and emotional harm. Many people who have accomplished significant goals in their lives still suffer low self-esteem and other mental and emotional harm.

Achievement is what you want and need in your life. All people should strive to reach their highest potential. But don't let your sense of self-worth depend on it. Be mindful that you need good self-esteem in the first place to take full advantage of your talent and the opportunities presented to you. Understand that you *can* feel good about yourself right here and right now, just as you are, no conditions attached, if you take the necessary action to protect yourself on the inside.

PROTECTION WITHIN YOUR CONTROL

You will appreciate that the strategy we recommend does not require the participation, permission, or approval of others. Many important civil-rights efforts in our society today are successful only if they can change certain laws or policies or transform the beliefs, attitudes, or behavior of others. When implementing this strategy, you do not have to change any people or occurrences outside of yourself. You do not have to increase your wealth or accomplish any external goals. All you have to do is change your understandings, beliefs, and perceptions. Everything you need to protect yourself on the inside is totally within your control.

COMMON PRACTICE

Using a strategy for your benefit in the living of your life is nothing out of the ordinary. Indeed, it is a practice with which most people are already familiar. Did your parents, grandparents, or others ever teach you certain rules and understandings about how to live your life? Did they advise you to treat others with dignity and respect, get a good education, work hard on your job, say your prayers, stand up for yourself, not steal from others, and the like? If others taught you certain rules and understandings about how to live your life, and you've followed those teachings, you already have the experience of using one or more strategies in your life to accomplish certain goals. Thus it is a natural progression to now use a strategy to protect yourself on the inside from the bigotry, prejudice, and other disrespect you encounter.

This Strategy Is Not for Everyone

For different reasons, not all people who suffer bigotry, prejudice, and other disrespect will implement a strategy to protect themselves on the inside. Despite all of the compelling reasons, some will still not appreciate the benefit of a strategy. Some will simply not do the work or exercise the discipline that is required. Some will perceive the strategy as a threat to (or betrayal of) existing practices and understandings. Of course, some may feel confident that they can effectively address mental and emotional harm caused by bigotry and prejudice on a case-by-case basis, without the benefit of any planning or forethought. But the mental and emotional harm to which you are exposed is too great to wait until it is directly upon you to decide what action to take to protect yourself. Public schools and other public places conduct fire drills to teach occupants how to get to safety in the event of a fire. During fire drills, occupants learn the best routes to safety. They appreciate that they are better able to escape harm if they know where the closest exits are and understand what precautions they must take before the fire begins. It is likewise when you encounter bigotry and prejudice. You are in a much better position to protect yourself on the inside from bigotry and prejudice if you have a well-considered plan before the bigotry and prejudice are committed against you.

If you feel you're doing just fine without a strategy to protect yourself, or if you already have a strategy of a different kind in place, we ask that you still consider what we have to offer. See for yourself whether you can, in any way, improve on what you are currently doing to enhance the quality of your life.

Recognize All Bigotry as a Lie

You MAY BE poor, unemployed, or homeless. You may not have the level of talent or ability that others may have. You may not perform as well as others on human-intelligence tests or other human evaluations. You may not have the physical body or the physical appearance that meets expectations. You may not have the material wealth that others may have. You may not have achieved in life or contributed to society at the same level as others. Some people may judge you as inferior based on your race, gender, religion, nationality, sexual orientation, or other social status. However, no matter what your achievement, social status, or other social identity may be, you are a valuable human being, just as valuable as anyone else in the world, and no person, occurrence, or thing can take that value away from you. No human being anywhere is inferior *or* superior in human value to any other human being, now or ever.

For sure, society has the right and responsibility to recognize, distinguish, reward, punish, and reprove individuals based on fair and just human measurements. But the judgment that some are more valuable as human beings than others goes too far and is not binding on you. That proposition is a fiction.

The human differences among people that some interpret as evidence of inferiority or superiority in human value are all swallowed up by the death of the physical body, that same death that we all must experience, each of us in our own time and place. It does not matter to death who you are, what you possess, what you have accomplished, or what value society may have assigned to your life. Certainly, you may leave behind material wealth, legacy, and memories for others to celebrate or enjoy, but for you personally, all material things end at the time of death.

If in the end everyone dies, does the bigot not spit in the wind when he or she insists that some lives are more valuable than other lives? Of course death is a future event, and you should be focused on living your life right now. However, your knowledge that death happens to everyone in the future is still a reality at this very moment. Although the act of death itself is in the future, you can use your knowledge of this future event *right now* to liberate yourself *right now* from the erroneous idea *right now* that some lives are more valuable than other lives.

By hope or faith, we and many others in our society, believe life continues in a different form after the death of the physical body. But if life continues after the death of the physical body, as some of us hope and believe, we already know we do not take the material world with us.

The people of this world are certainly different in many ways. These differences absolutely play a tremendous role in the way we live our lives, if we let them, but they do not define human value. As human beings we are still more alike than we are different. We all enter into the world through the experience of birth. We all need oxygen, food, and shelter to live. We all live in communities. We all want to be loved and respected. We all have fears and anxieties. We all are vulnerable to illness or disease. And we all die.

The proposition that some people are more valuable than others as human beings is nothing more than a *belief*, and like many beliefs, it has no power, no substance, and no meaning on its own. It has meaning only if people believe it is true.

The mythical bogeyman has much to teach about bigotry and prejudice in society. A young child may be concerned that the bogeyman hides at night in the closet or underneath the bed. In truth there is no bogeyman. But the bogeyman still causes fear and fear-based behavior for those who believe he is real. Bigotry and prejudice operate in the same manner. Although superiority or inferiority in human value is an illusion, bigots who believe it is true are inclined to react with fear and deny others their rights and privileges. A person who experiences bigotry and prejudice and also believes the illusion is real, will likely suffer mental and emotional harm. But if you see the illusion for what it is, it will no longer have the power to hurt you on the inside as it did before.

Of course, your personal understanding that the illusion is just that will not change the attitudes or behavior of others. Others will continue to assess human value as they see fit. Others will continue to perpetrate bigotry and prejudice against you. Your liberation from mental and emotional harm will not come from a change in others but from your understanding of your value as a human being.

Every act of bigotry you experience, every implied or explicit statement that you are inferior as a human being, is composed of two parts. The first part is the statement that you do not meet certain standards. The second part is a conclusion based on the first part: that because you do not meet certain standards, you are inferior. Thus the act of bigotry operates as an equation: The failure to meet certain standards equals inferiority. But this equation is a fallacy. Your failure, if any, to meet certain standards does not equal inferiority, because inferiority in human value does not exist in the first place. Remember, no human being anywhere is inferior in human value to any other human being.

Of course, meeting certain standards in society is not unimportant. Most of us understand the importance of law-abiding behavior and good citizenship. You want to do your very best to achieve at a high level in education, employment, living conditions, professional development, and other important areas of life. But in all of your efforts and desires to achieve and meet standards in life, you must be mindful that your success or lack of success in these matters does not define your value as a human being.

Some may argue that if a sense of self-worth were not based on meeting valuable standards, the motivation to meet these standards would be diminished. But how stable can any motivation be if it is based on the uncertainty and fear of achieving things in order to feel good about yourself? Motivation to achieve should arise not out of fear but out of passion, inspiration, and a sense of responsibility. People should not strive to reach a certain level of achievement in order for them to be considered worthy human beings. They must understand that they are already worthy human beings and achievement should not play a role in their sense of self-worth.

When someone commits an act of bigotry against you, thereby stating or implying you do not meet certain standards or expectations, you may want to defend yourself against this accusation. If you meet the standards the bigot says you don't meet, you may want to set the record straight, whether directly with the bigot or in your own mind. If you do not meet the bigot's standards, you may argue that the standards are unfair, or you might even state reasons justifying your failure to meet those standards. You may say something like the following:

> That's an insult; you do know that, don't you? Where did you get your information anyway? All black people are *not* on welfare. There are more white people on welfare than blacks. Black people would not be on welfare in the first place if they had equal rights.

If you are currently defending your sense of self-worth by debating your ability or inability to meet certain standards or expectations, you need to change your narrative. From this day forward, whenever you experience an act of bigotry or prejudice, you should totally dismiss standards and expectations when defending the attack against you. If you need to improve your life in some way as suggested by the bigot, you certainly should consider doing so. However, that issue of self-improvement is a different matter altogether. Whether you decide to improve your life or not should have nothing to do with the bigot's suggestion. Self-improvement is your own personal matter. Do not let the bigot trick you into believing standards and expectations define your value as a human being.

If you feel you must address standards and expectations when the bigot commits bigotry against you, certainly you should go ahead and do so. Just be careful that you do not deceive yourself in the process. Keep in mind that you do not need to prove or justify anything with regard to your equality or value as a human being. Your value as a human being was permanently established by your birth into the world, and no person or people, thing, or occurrence can take your value away from you.

No matter your outward response, whenever someone commits an act of bigotry against you, mentally you must accomplish two very important things. You must (1) recognize the bigot's claim that you do not meet certain standards as totally irrelevant, because meeting or not meeting certain standards proves nothing with regard to your value as a human being; and (2) remind yourself that the proposition that some people are inferior to others is an illusion that exists only in the minds of the misguided. You can accomplish both of these objectives with a simple, lighthearted jingle.

Notice that the bogeyman jingle provided above is silent with regard to whether you meet certain standards or expectations. The silence on this matter is your reminder that expectations and standards do not speak to your value as a human being. The words of the jingle are your reminder that any belief that one human being is superior to another human being is an illusion.

If the bogeyman jingle does not feel right for you, remind yourself of the important understandings you need to remember in whatever manner you choose. For example, you could just say the words of the jingle and not sing them. Or you could simply say to yourself, *There is no bogeyman.* You might even say, *There is no such thing as some people being more valuable than others.* Whatever words you use, be brief and to the point. Follow the example of the bogeyman jingle, and include nothing regarding your ability or inability to meet certain standards and expectations.

An alternative to the bogeyman jingle is certainly an option. However, we highly recommend the bogeyman jingle. Give the jingle an opportunity to grow on you as a fun and effective way to protect yourself on the inside.

Sing the bogeyman jingle to yourself whenever someone commits an act of bigotry or prejudice against you. Repeat it as many times as you need. Sometimes, you may choose to sing the jingle out loud if you feel further strengthened by doing so. Also, you may, if you dare, choose to say or sing the words directly to the bigot to confront him in his behavior. Keep in mind, however, that the primary purpose of the jingle is to protect yourself from mental and emotional harm. It does not take the place of confrontation. Thus, in addition to the bogeyman jingle, you must continue to confront the bigot about his harmful behavior. (More about openly confronting the bigot follows later in this book, in "Don't Debate the Lie.")

Your consistent and repeated use of the bogeyman jingle will instill in you a new understanding of the act of bigotry. This new understanding will protect you from mental and emotional harm. All bigotry against you is a lie because all bigotry states or implies that you are inferior as a human being when that is absolutely not the case. The bigot commits bigotry against you in an effort to trick you into swallowing the lie that there is a bogeyman who has hurt you and is treating you unkindly. In truth, the bogeyman has not hurt you; the bogeyman does not even exist. When you understand these important truths about bigotry, bigotry loses its mental and emotional power over you and does not hurt you on the inside in the same way it has in the past.

The bigotry that you encounter in your life takes many different forms and comes at unexpected times and in unexpected places. Thus, if you anticipate the specific ways bigotry arises in everyday life, you are in a much better position to remember to use the bogeyman jingle as recommended.

PHYSICAL ASSAULT AND DENIAL OF RIGHTS AND PRIVILEGES

If someone assaults you physically or denies you your rights and privileges, using the bogeyman jingle to protect yourself from mental and emotional harm probably will not be your first priority. If you do remember to use the jingle while you experience this bigoted act or shortly thereafter, that's great. If not, certainly there will be other opportunities in the days that follow.

Protecting yourself from mental and emotional harm does not in any way replace the other important things that you must do to stand up for yourself and exercise your legal and human rights. So when someone assaults you physically or denies you your legal or human rights, matters such as protecting your physical body, taking care of any physical injuries sustained, obtaining compensation or other remedies to which you are entitled, and holding the perpetrators accountable may be foremost on your mind. However, at some point after the assault or denial has been perpetrated against you, you will remember that you also need to protect yourself from the loss of self-esteem and other mental and emotional harm that these assaults have caused.

Hopefully, you will never suffer a bigoted assault or a bigoted denial of your rights and or privileges. But if the bigot does attack you in this way, say or think the bogeyman jingle to yourself as soon as you remember to do so, and continue to use it this way as a protection throughout your recovery and beyond.

Especially after a physical assault against you or the denial of your rights and privileges, you need to know the wrong against you says absolutely nothing about your value as a human being. You need to know you are a valuable human being, just a valuable as anyone and everyone else in the world, and no person or people, thing, or occurrence can take that away from you.

Bigotry in Everyday Communication

Bigoted name-calling, bigoted words and phrases, and bigoted statements and questions in everyday language, whether they are written or spoken, state or imply that you are inferior because you do not meet certain standards or expectations. When you truly recognize these words and phrases as a lie, they no longer have the power or authority to hurt you on the inside. Certainly you and others will continue in your efforts to stop all bigotry and prejudice in our society. Meanwhile, until that day comes when everyone is treated with dignity and respect, use the bogeyman jingle to protect yourself on the inside from everyday communications that state or imply you are inferior.

Exclusion

A coworker invites everyone at the office, except you, to attend his birthday party at his home. A member of your book group is very friendly and engaging to everyone in the group except you. A leader in a civic organization of which you are a member consistently asks others to join committees to do the work of the organization, but never invites you. Incidents of exclusion such as the examples described here, when based on bigotry or prejudice, imply you are inferior in value as a human being because you do not meet certain standards or expectations.

In most cases of exclusion, the bigot will not actually say he or she is excluding you based on bigotry. Indeed, if asked, the bigot will often deny bigotry is the motivation. In the interest of self-integrity and fairness to others, you have to be discerning about these types of situations. In general, however, you know when people have prejudice against you, even when they deny it, and you can sense that your race kept you out of the birthday party or your religion denied you a friendship in the book club or your nationality prevented you from fuller involvement in a civic organization.

Sometimes when you are excluded, a legal remedy may be available to you. In addition, you may choose to confront the person who has excluded you. However, whether or not any action is taken against the perpetrator, you must recognize the lie for what it is and use the bogeyman jingle to protect yourself on the inside.

Injection of Roles or Identities

Sometimes misguided people will inject gender, ethnicity, or other roles and identities into a conversation when such roles and identities are totally irrelevant to the subject being discussed. As an example, consider the following hypothetical situation. A thirty-five-year-old white male named Arnold is at a dinner party. During the party, Arnold says, "I drove down to New York City on business the other day, and on my way back, this woman state trooper pulled me over and gave me a speeding ticket." In this particular example, Arnold is truthful in his statement that a female state trooper pulled him over and gave him a speeding ticket. But what difference does it make that the state trooper is a woman?

In many everyday communications in society, reference to gender, race, nationality, or other roles and identities is absolutely necessary. But in some communications, the injection of roles or identities does nothing but imply certain groups are inferior. Did Arnold in the hypothetical example described here imply women state troopers are inferior when he brought gender into the conversation? Some may say yes; others may say no. But what if Arnold said a black state trooper had pulled him over and gave him a ticket? Or what if he said a Puerto Rican state trooper or a gay state trooper had pulled him over and gave him a ticket?

If you are hurt on the inside when someone injects gender, ethnicity, or other roles or identities into a conversation, when the roles or identities injected are totally irrelevant to the topic at hand, just remind yourself that you have encountered the lie of bigotry. Use the bogeyman jingle to protect yourself on the inside.

Stereotypes

Stereotypes are beliefs or assumptions commonly held in the general population about certain groups based on race, ethnic background, religion, gender, sexual orientation, or other social identities. For example, the belief or assumption that white people don't have rhythm is a stereotype. The belief or assumption that black people do have rhythm is a stereotype. Stereotypes can be positive or negative. The belief or assumption that people of a certain race will honor their commitments is an example of a positive stereotype. The belief or assumption that people of a certain race will not honor their commitments is an example of a negative stereotype.

The problem with stereotypes is that some of them are inaccurate in how they portray the groups to which they apply. And all stereotypes, whether accurate or not, do not apply to everyone in the group, and they often deny people who happen to belong to certain groups the privilege of individuality. In addition, there are explanations or justifications for some negative stereotypes that the general public does not understand or appreciate.

Some people use stereotypes with reckless disregard for others or with the specific intent to cause others mental or emotional harm. Some use stereotypes with no harm or disrespect intended. Whatever the motivation of the perpetrator, stereotypes can be harmful mentally or emotionally. Therefore, we must continue in our work to stop or discourage the use of stereotypes altogether.

Every stereotype used against you, whether accurate or inaccurate, negative or positive, is an implied or explicit statement about whether your group meets certain standards or expectations. But standards and expectations do not define your value as a human being. Accordingly, whenever you are insulted or otherwise bothered by a stereotype against you, use the bogeyman jingle to protect yourself on the inside.

DISPARITIES SUFFERED BY THE GROUP OR GROUPS TO WHICH YOU BELONG

If you do not understand or remember the truth about your value as a human being, information about the disparities that your racial, ethnic, or other social groups suffer will cause you loss of self-esteem and other mental and emotional harm. For example, do you feel diminished or threatened on the inside by statistics that show people of your racial or ethnic group die of natural causes at a younger age than others in the general population? Do you feel diminished or threatened on the inside by statistics that show the people of your racial or ethnic group more frequently live in poverty, achieve poorly in education, experience unemployment, have low-paying jobs, or spend time in prison than others in the general population? Do you feel diminished or threatened on the inside by reports that state that people of your racial or ethnic group suffer diabetes, high blood pressure, strokes, or other medical conditions more than others in the general population? Even if the disparities suffered by your social group or groups do not pertain to you personally, do you still identify with these groups and feel diminished or threatened on the inside by association?

We must continue our work to eliminate the disparities that many people suffer. We must continue to reject any malicious or misguided ideas about who or what caused these disparities. At the same time, it is critical that you understand and remember that the disparities suffered by your particular group or groups can hurt you on the inside *only* if you let them.

Disparities suffered by you or the group or groups to which you belong do not determine your value as a human being. Therefore, you do not have to justify yourself or wait until such disparities have been re-solved to feel good about yourself. You are a valuable human being right here and right now, no conditions attached.

Some people use information about the disparities you or your groups suffer as an instrument to try to put you down. Of course, many other people use such information routinely for good and necessary purposes with no harm or disrespect intended. Whatever the case may be, whenever you feel diminished or otherwise threatened on the inside by disparities suffered by you or any social groups to which you belong, use the bogeyman jingle to protect yourself from mental and emotional harm.

Other Bigotry, Prejudice, and Disrespect

Do you feel diminished or threatened on the inside by your general knowledge that in this society there is prejudice against you, even when you are not personally experiencing any specific acts of bigotry or preju-dice at the time? If so, use the bogeyman jingle to protect yourself on the inside.

Perhaps you experience the lie of bigotry in one or more ways not specifically described in this book. If so, use the bogeyman jingle to protect yourself on the inside. Don't be deceived by the many subtle or underhanded ways people use bigotry against you. Subtle bigotry can be just as harmful as any other kind.

As you use the bogeyman jingle to protect yourself from mental and emotional harm, you are not obliged to tell anyone what you are doing to improve the quality of your life. However, you may choose to share this important practice with people who are open and receptive to what you're doing, especially if this practice could benefit them as well. Just be mindful that it is not necessary that you convince anyone of the truth or defend or justify what you're doing. Above all, you do not have to convince the bigot. In fact, you probably would not be able to convince the bigot anyway, no matter what you say or do, because what you are doing threatens the bigot. Surely, you are not trying to keep the bogeyman jingle secret. If you find yourself talking with the bigot about the boogeyman jingle or other related issues, that's not a problem. Just remember you do not need the bigot's agreement to protect yourself from mental or emotional harm. All you have to do is understand for yourself the value of what you're doing.

The first few times you use the bogeyman jingle, you may not immediately notice a difference in your life. If so, don't be concerned. Just keep doing what you're doing. As you continue to use the jingle over a period of time, you will become increasingly stronger and more confident in your ability to protect yourself from mental and emotional harm caused by bigotry.

Ideally, you want to say or think the bogeyman jingle at the very moment bigotry is committed against you, or immediately afterward. But this is not always possible. In the heat of battle, sometimes you will not remember the jingle until well after the act of indignity has been committed against you. If so, do not beat yourself up. Later on, you will remember you're dealing with the lie of bigotry. When you do remember, just say or think the jingle at that time.

You will probably find yourself reciting the boogeyman jingle mostly to yourself. However, as you feel comfortable in doing so, say it or sing it out loud around others. Use the jingle generously, even when no specific act of bigotry or other disrespect has been committed against you. Sing it, for example, before you enter into a meeting or other gathering where some people in attendance may harbor prejudice against you. Civil-rights activists of the past often joined together singing the song, "We Shall Overcome." In a similar manner, you can join together with others in singing the bogeyman jingle aloud at protest activities or during other similar gatherings to support and uplift one another.

Use the bogeyman jingle when you are feeling low. Use it when you're feeling fine. There are no harmful side effects. Use it repeatedly in your life, and you will grow increasingly stronger against anyone or anything that would threaten your sense of your value as a human being. Let the boogeyman jingle be your constant companion.

Awaken to the Bigot's Motivation

WITHOUT A DOUBT, the bigot is an integral part of the overall act of bigotry. Bigotry itself causes the loss of self-esteem and other mental and emotional harm you suffer. But the bigot is the perpetrator of this indignity. Therefore, to protect yourself from mental and emotional harm, you must address not only the act of bigotry but also the person who commits bigotry against you.

If you do nothing to protect yourself from bigots, they will frighten you, intimidate you, threaten you, generate hostility within you, and mentally and emotionally haunt you. This will impair and diminish the overall quality of your life until you die. But there is much you can do and should do to prevent bigots from harming you in this way.

Bigots can hurt you mentally and emotionally only if they have some measure of credibility with you. For example, a person who cannot find her or his own way out of the forest has absolutely no credibility when criticizing hikers nearby for being lost. It is likewise with bigots. Bigots are struggling mightily with their own sense of self-worth. They have no authority to declare others as inferior.

Essentially, bigots perpetrate bigotry against you out of their own fears and feelings of inadequacy. Of course, if you ask bigots why they harbor prejudice against other people, they would probably say things such as, "they're inferior," "they're lazy," "they're irresponsible," "they're immoral," "they're dishonest," and the like. But when bigots respond in this way, they are only giving their justifications. Their justifications do not explain why they behave as they do.

Bigots think they are better than other people. And most people understand that. But even if they were better than other people, why would they hate others? Why would they despise or disparage them? Why would they exclude others or otherwise deny them their legal and human rights? Bigots have options. They could sympathize with those they deem inferior or even help those people in their situations. In some cases, if bigots chose not to help, they could just walk away. But they do not walk away. They do not offer help or sympathy of any kind. They are committed to one path and one path only. They act repeatedly to try to put others down.

Don't let anybody fool you. If a bigot comes after you peddling bigotry and prejudice in an effort to put you down, he or she does so for a reason. To fully understand a bigot's motivation, you have to ask yourself, "What's in it for the bigot? What does a bigot get out of it when he or she tries to put me down? How does the bigot benefit?"

Sadly, a huge component of bigots' sense of self-worth is based on how they see themselves as compared to how they see others. They constantly compare what they perceive as their value as a human being to what they perceive as the value of others. If they can establish and maintain in their own minds that they are superior to the "inferior" people of the world, they feel good about themselves and deem themselves valuable human beings. Any idea or suggestion that the "inferior" people of the world are equal in value to them is a threat to their sense of self-worth. Thus, bigots find themselves operating out of fear. They feel that if they are not better than the "inferior" people of the world, they are not worth much of anything themselves.

By the way, you don't need scientific study or "expert" testimony to know a bigot's motivation. You can understand a bigot's motivation based on your personal observations and common-sense understanding of human behavior. You know, for example, with no outside proof necessary, that the neighborhood bully intimidates and assaults others in an effort to feel good about himself or herself. You know it because you know it. If you can understand the bully's motivation without scientific study or expert testimony, you can certainly understand the motivation of the bigot. Indeed, the bigot *is* the bully on the playground, hurting others in order to feel good about himself or herself.

Of course, some bigots also use bigotry for financial, political, or other material gain. But material gain is not a different motivation; it is just an extension of the same. The bottom line is that the motivation of bigots is to advance or protect their own misguided sense of self-worth. When material advantage is also available, they do not resist the temptation.

The fundamental flaw in bigots' way of thinking is their belief that some people in society are more valuable than others as human beings. As previously stated, inequality in human value is an illusion, and those who believe in this illusion are like uninformed individuals who believe the bogeyman is real.

Bigots believe strongly in the bogeyman and are not willing to give up the illusion. They use the bogeyman to feel good about themselves. In their own minds, when the bogeyman declares others inferior, they themselves (bigots) are lifted up and distinguished as valuable. But bigots live in fear. They are frightened that they could become victims of the bogeyman, and they also fear that one day, society may awaken to the truth that the bogeyman is indeed an illusion.

When you understand and remember that bigots are not as strong and secure on the inside as they pretend to be on the outside, and when you understand and remember that they are operating out of fear and feelings of inadequacy, bigots lose credibility with you and do not have the influence to intimidate you or cause you mental and emotional harm in the same way or to the same extent as they did before. You will see bigots as people who are trying desperately to maintain their own sense of self-worth and who do not have the integrity or credibility to declare you as inferior. You will see bigots as people who are severely compromised by their own vulnerability.

Of course, bigots may still have the power to harm you physically or take away your rights and privileges. Therefore, you must continue to protect your physical body at all times. You must continue to stand up for your rights and privileges. But still, whatever harm or denial bigots commit against you, they can no longer hurt you on the inside as they did before.

You must intentionally use your understanding of the bigots' vulnerability to protect yourself from mental and emotional harm. But merely entertaining the thought that bigots have fears and feelings of inadequacy is not enough to protect you. You must go further and actually implement the truth about the bigot totally and completely into your way of thinking. In the same way that you now have the bogeyman jingle to remind you that all bigotry is a lie, you also need a tool to remind you that bigots are not as strong and secure as they pretend, but that they are frightened and desperate with regard to their sense of self-worth.

Certainly, as a society we already have words in place to describe bigots. Not only do we call them "bigots," but we sometimes call them "sexist" or "homophobic," for example, depending on the category of their bigoted behavior. These labels tell us that bigots hate. But they do not address bigots' fears and lack of credibility.

Bigots are in a very difficult situation without an easy way to escape, except to give up bigotry altogether. Metaphorically speaking, they are "up a tree." They do not want you to know they put other people down in order to feel good about themselves, but this is precisely what they are telling you every time they commit bigotry against you. Therefore, it is fitting to use the "up a tree" metaphor as your reminder that bigots are compromised with regard to any mental or emotional authority that they believe they have over you.

Whenever a bigot commits an act of bigotry against you or whenever you are angered, frightened, intimidated, hurt, or otherwise bothered in any way by a bigot, think or say to yourself, "That bigot's up a tree." Use your imagination to see that the bigot is up in the tree, stationed there in fear and anxiety. Sometimes, but not always, bigots take rocks up into the tree with them and throw these rocks at people below. The rock-throwing part is your reminder that although bigots are frightened and insecure, they still may be harmful. Therefore, you must protect yourself at all times.

After you have a bigot up a tree in your imagination, you can go further and try to talk the bigot down. To be clear, you would not literally try to talk him or her down, at least not in all cases. The bigot climbed the tree in your imagination. Accordingly, you would try to talk her down in your imagination by saying or thinking to yourself:

> *Hey, [Sue]. Come down out of that tree.*
> *And stop throwing those rocks,*
> *you could hurt somebody.*
> *You don't have to throw rocks at other people*
> *to feel good about yourself; you never did.*
> *So stop throwing those rocks*
> *And come down out of that tree.*

If, in your imagination, the bigot does not come down from the tree as you have requested, that's not a problem. Your only concern at the moment is that you invited him or her to come down. The process alone of trying to talk the bigot down enhances your perception of him or her as an individual who absolutely does not have the authority or credibility to judge you as inferior in value as a human being.

When talking the bigot down, you do not have to use the precise language provided in the example above. If the precise language in the example works for you, that's fine. If not, be creative and come up with your own words. However, be certain to maintain the integrity of the example. Also, don't just say the words for the sake of saying them. Be focused and very much aware of what you are saying or thinking to yourself. You want to talk the bigot down in a firm but lighthearted manner. You want to have no anger, resentment, or hostility of any kind. The bigot, after all, is a frightened individual who should not be up a tree in that way.

In total, you now have three ways in which to use the "up a tree" metaphor to protect yourself from bigots. First, say or think to yourself,

"That person is up a tree." Second, use your imagination to envision the bigot up a tree. Third, with the bigot up the tree in your imagination, use your imagination to try to talk the bigot down. Ideally, you want to use all three ways to the fullest extent possible. But if you cannot use all three all of the time, use one or more to the best of your ability.

Sometimes certain social or political groups will commit bigotry or express bigoted attitudes against you or the group or groups to which you belong. Whenever one or more social groups have committed prejudice against you, use the "up a tree" metaphor to protect yourself on the inside. In your imagination, tell the group members they are up in a tree. See the individual members up in different trees and try to talk them down. Perhaps you see one in each tree in a forest. Or as you are driving your car to work or other destinations, you notice different trees along the way, and each tree has two or three group members clinging there to the tree limbs. Well, don't just leave them there. In your imagination, try to talk them down.

> Hey, people. Come down out of those trees.
> And stop throwing those rocks,
> you could hurt somebody.
> You don't have to throw rocks at other people
> to feel good about yourselves; you never did.
> So stop throwing those rocks
> And come down out of those trees.

In addition, sometimes a bigot out of your past will reappear to disturb you today on the inside. If so, go ahead and try to talk this individual down out of the tree, to help yourself in moving on beyond the hurt you experienced.

> Hey, [Jim]. Are you still up in that tree
> throwing rocks at people?
> If you are, you have to come down.
> Stop throwing those rocks,

you could hurt somebody.
You don't have to throw rocks at other people
to feel good about yourself; you never did.
So stop throwing those rocks
And come down out of that tree.

Whether you should tell others what you're doing to protect yourself from bigots is a matter of personal discretion. Use the same discretion you apply when considering whether to disclose your use of the bogeyman jingle. The guiding principle is that you do not have to *literally* tell bigots, or anyone else, that you are using the "up a tree" metaphor. Of course, you may choose to share this information with certain people who are open and receptive to what you're doing, especially if the metaphor could benefit them as well. Also, on some selected occasions, you may choose to *literally* invite a bigot to come down out of the tree just to tell the bigot a few things about himself or herself. But still you do not have to convince anyone of the truth of the metaphor or defend or justify what you're doing. Above all, you do not have to convince the bigot. You probably would not be able to convince a bigot anyway, no matter what you say, because what you are doing threatens the bigot's illusion. You do not need the bigot's agreement to protect yourself on the inside. All you have to do is understand and appreciate in your mind the value of what you're doing.

The bottom line is that the "up a tree" metaphor could be your personal secret, or a practice you share with family members and friends. Or you could be very open to everyone, including the bigot, about what you're doing. It's entirely up to you.

The "up a tree" metaphor operates in many ways like the bogeyman jingle. The first few times you use the metaphor, you may perceive an immediate difference in your life, but not necessarily. If you do not perceive immediate results, don't be concerned. Just stay with what you're doing. As you continue to use the metaphor over a period of time, you will become increasingly stronger on the inside against anyone and everyone who tries to put you down.

Your goal is to use the metaphor as a protection at the very moment bigots commit bigotry against you, or soon thereafter. But this is not always possible. In the heat of battle, sometimes you will not remember to apply the metaphor until well after the indignity has been committed. If so, that's not a problem. At some point after you have experienced the indignity, you *will* remember to protect yourself. Use the metaphor once you remember.

Use the "up a tree" metaphor not only when bigots commit specific acts of bigotry against you, but whenever you feel threatened, angered, frightened, intimidated, or otherwise bothered by them in any way. Talk bigots down when you're feeling low. Talk bigots down when you're feeling fine. Be very generous in using this important tool to protect yourself from mental and emotional harm, and be as lighthearted as possible in the overall process.

Whatever money, power, status, or other privilege bigots may have, they are still troubled individuals on the inside. Otherwise, they would not come after you. But they *do* come after you and try to put you down in a misguided effort to protect and enhance their own sense of self-worth. For sure, they can still harm you physically. They can still deny you your rights and privileges. But their ability to harm you mentally and emotionally has been compromised and diminished in a significant way by your understanding of their fears and feelings of inadequacy. Use the "up a tree" metaphor to make your understandings of bigots come alive within and greatly improve the overall quality of your life.

As you continue to use the "up a tree" metaphor over a period of time, you will see bigots more clearly each day for what they are—troubled, misguided individuals who are lost and perhaps someday will be found. For now, understand that they are up in trees without the credibility or integrity to intimidate, anger, frighten, or otherwise hurt you on the inside in the same way as they did before. But be careful that you do not judge bigots harshly or harbor anger or resentment against them. See them for what they truly are, but do not harbor negative feelings. When you harbor hostility, you only hurt or limit yourself.

Detach from Your Roles and Identities

WHENEVER BIGOTS COMMIT bigotry or harbor prejudice against you, they can hurt you mentally or emotionally only if you believe you are inferior or have some measure of doubt about your value as a human being. "No one can make you feel inferior without your consent," is a statement often attributed to First Lady Eleanor Roosevelt, the wife of Franklin D. Roosevelt, the thirty-second president of the United States. This very insightful statement speaks the truth. To what extent do you judge yourself as inferior or have some measure of doubt about your value as a human being?

If you are as strong as you need to be in your belief that you are as valuable as anyone and everyone else in the world, no bigots would ever be able to hurt you mentally or emotionally. This is not to say that everyone who's been hurt on the inside by bigotry or prejudice has bad self-esteem—not at all. Many who are hurt on the inside by the bigotry of others have good self-esteem. Many truly believe they are inferior to no one. But how strong are you in that belief? If you are as strong as you need to be, you would not feel *any* mental or emotional hurt when someone puts you down. The truth of the matter is that if you are still being hurt on the inside by the bigotry and disrespect of others, there are opportunities to improve the quality of your life.

The only way anyone, including you, can ever judge you as inferior is by finding fault with your race, religion, gender, national origin, sexual orientation, economic status, or any of the other roles that have been assigned to you in life. If you take your roles and identities out of the equation, there is nothing left upon which people can judge you as inferior.

Therefore, if you're judging yourself as inferior or having doubt about your value as a human being, stop judging your own value based on your roles and identities.

Of course, if you stop judging your human value based on your roles and identities, it is likely that society in general will not be impressed. The general public will continue to believe and behave as though your roles and identities do reflect your value as a human being. But what society believes and how society behaves is not binding on what you believe. Your roles and identities will determine your value as a human being only if you say so. It is entirely up to you.

Your race is your race, but you are not your race. Your gender is your gender, but you are not your gender. Your nationality, religion, occupation, educational degrees, economic status, sexual orientation, and any of your other roles and identities are indeed yours, but you are not they. You are a valuable human being who uses or tolerates the different roles and identities assigned to you in your life.

It makes no difference how you may have acquired any of your roles or identities. Some, like your race and gender, were with you at the time of your birth. You may have acquired others by hard work and dedication. Some may come to you due to bad choices, lack of effort, or bad luck. Whatever the case may be, you are not your roles and identities.

This is not to say that roles and identities are not unimportant nor to say that you should deny any of them. Indeed, some of your roles and identities are extremely important to you. Some actually function as the very tools you use to live a productive and satisfying life.

If you like your race and choose to embrace it, go ahead and embrace it, but do so with the understanding that your race is not who or what you are. If you like your job or profession and choose to embrace it, go ahead and embrace it, but do so with the understanding that your job or profession is not who or what you are. If you like your national origin and choose to embrace it, go ahead and embrace it, but do so with the understanding that your national origin is not who or what you are. Embrace any or all of your roles and identities if that's what you choose to do. Take pride in your achievement, take pride in your social status, take pride in your possessions, if that's what you choose to do, but don't go so far that you interpret these things as the essence of who you are. You are *not* your roles or identities, and your roles and identities do not define you or determine your value as a human being.

Seeing yourself and others as separate and distinct from your roles and identities is definitely not a new or novel idea that originated with us. Actually, there is a specific word that one can use to describe this awareness: "detachment." To stop basing your value as a human being on your roles and identities is to detach from them.

Detachment for some is an important religious belief. For example, the Christian Bible separates the Spirit from the physical body and further states that the Spirit should prevail over the body. The Apostle Paul writes in Galatians 5:16–17, "Live by the Spirit, I say, and do not gratify the desires of the flesh. For what the flesh desires is opposed to the Spirit, and what the Spirit desires is opposed to the flesh; for these are opposed to each other, to prevent you from doing what you want."

Many people who show no partiality to any specific religious practice also believe in detachment. Some in this category frequently say the phrase, "I am a spiritual being having a human experience" or words to that effect. Perhaps you have heard this expression yourself or possibly seen it on a poster or bumper sticker.

Without a doubt, different people have embraced detachment for centuries as an important religious belief or a helpful spiritual practice. You can now use this same important practice as an instrument to help liberate yourself mentally and emotionally from the bigotry, prejudice, and other disrespect you encounter in your life.

If you find yourself struggling with the concept of detachment, an analogy involving a car may be helpful. Imagine that you own several cars that are all parked in a spacious garage. You inherited some of these cars at the time of your birth. Others were given to you, or you acquired them later in life. Some of your cars are very important to you, and you admire them, enjoy them, and use them to take you to where you need and want to go. Other cars you own are not so important, and perhaps you would like to improve them, discard them, or even change some people's negative attitudes about them. But no matter how important or unimportant any of your cars may be, you are not your cars.

It is likewise with your roles and identities. Some of your roles and identities are very important to you, and you admire them, enjoy them, and use them to accomplish important things in your life. At the same time, you may have other roles and identities that are not important or may even be harmful. Perhaps you would like to change or discard some of your roles and identities or change society's negative attitudes about them. But no matter how important or unimportant any of your roles or identities may be, you are not your roles and identities.

Detachment does not mean indifference. You will continue to take action to protect and enhance those roles and identities that are important to you. You will continue your hard work to destroy all bigotry and prejudice. If some or even all of your roles and identities are just as valuable as the roles and identities of others, you should certainly feel free to say so.

If your race is just as valuable as your neighbor's race, go ahead and say so. If your religion is just as valuable as other religions, say it is so. If your gender is just as valuable as another gender, speak the truth about it. Say it loudly. Say it clearly. Say it to yourself. Say it to others. And when you have some roles and identities, such "poor person" or "unemployed person," that you would prefer not to have, you should certainly feel free to justify to yourself or others why this is so. However, when you practice detachment and take action to protect or enhance certain roles and identities, you do so to create better living conditions for yourself and others. When you practice detachment, you are not trying to prove your self-worth based on your roles and identities, because you understand that your roles and identities are not who or what you are. After all, through the practice of attachment you now understand that they do not determine your value as a human being.

Obviously, the integration of detachment into your personal life will not change other people. Others will continue to identify people based on their roles and identities. Others will continue to use different labels to describe people, labels such as "teacher," "nurse," "black woman," "plumber," "minority member," and so forth. Indeed, roles and identities are vital in the current process of how humans communicate with each other, and it would be impractical to try to exclude roles and identities from everyday language. So we don't recommend going around challenging people every time they refer to you as one or more of your roles or identities. Certainly, you, too, will continue to use roles and identities to identify yourself and others when it makes sense to do so. However, through the practice of detachment, when you use roles and identities in your everyday life, or encounter others doing so, you will remember and understand that people are *not* the roles they play.

Detachment brings about a major shift in your way of thinking. For example, if your occupation is university professor, others may call you "Professor" and sometimes you may call yourself "Professor," but university professor is not who or what you are. If society identifies you as a white male, others may call you a white male, and sometimes you may call yourself a white male, but white male is not who or what you are. If you recently immigrated to the United States to escape war or other misfortune, others may identify you as an immigrant, and sometimes you may identify yourself as an immigrant, but immigrant is not who or what you are.

The black woman who waved to you this morning as you were entering the grocery store is not a black woman. She is a valuable human being playing the role of a black woman until that role is over. The senator you saw on television yesterday giving a campaign speech is not a senator, but a valuable human being playing the role of a senator until that role is over. If you are a homeless person on the street, you are in truth not a homeless person on the street. Instead, you are a valuable human being playing the role of a homeless person until that role is over.

Undeniably, some of the roles that people play in society are very real with very definite and unambiguous consequences. Make no mistake about that. But people nonetheless are not the roles they play. You and others everywhere are valuable human beings playing different roles in society until those roles are over.

You Are Not Your Car

Earlier we recommended that you use the bogeyman jingle to remind yourself of the truths about bigotry. We also recommended the "up a tree" metaphor as your reminder of the bigot's motivation to put you down. We now recommend that you use the car analogy to remind you that you are not your roles and identities.

Be mindful that any particular role or identity you may have is like your car, which, you know, is not you. Likewise, your roles or identities are not you. To make detachment come alive in your life, we recommend that you adopt the slogan, "I am not my car," or "you are not your car," as your constant companion. Say or think the slogan to yourself on a regular basis. Use it especially when you (or others you encounter) appear to be overwhelmed by or dominated by the belief that you (or they) are the roles you (or they) play.

When getting dressed in the morning to start your day, look at yourself in the mirror, and say to yourself, "OK, but I am not my car." You may also say the slogan to yourself at other times during the day.

If a high-performing coworker thinks of himself as a privileged person and behaves as if you and certain other "unimportant" employees do not exist, tell this individual in your mind, "OK, but you are not your car."

If you have friends or family members who speak constantly of the bigotry and prejudice that they experience in their lives and are obsessed with seeing themselves as victims, tell them in the privacy of your mind, "OK, but you are not your car."

If you see on television people of local, national, or international fame who are totally impressed with themselves as celebrities, tell them in your mind, "OK, but you are not your car."

Throughout each day, when you notice a black man being a black man, a mayor being a mayor, a poor person being a poor person, a bank manger being a bank manager, an immigrant being an immigrant, an African being an African, an Italian American being an Italian American, a white woman being a white woman, a billionaire being a billionaire, or whatever the case may be, say to the individual in your mind, "OK, but you are not your car." Of course, you would not repeat the slogan *every time* you notice another person in the world. That would not be realistic or practical. It is sufficient if you use the slogan on a regular and persistent basis to remind yourself to detach from your roles and identities.

Say the slogan to different people whether you know them well or only by acquaintance, whether you know them by word-of-mouth or only from television, radio, or other public media. In doing so, you will find yourself using the slogan in your encounters with coworkers, celebrities, family members, friends, neighbors, fellow shoppers, members of the staff at your doctor's office or dentist's office, fellow worshipers at church, government officials, public-transportation employees, state and federal employees, cashiers and other employees at grocery stores or department stores, town residents at town meetings, and so forth.

Since you engage people with the slogan in your mind, the people you engage do not have to be *physically* in your presence at the time of the encounter. On those occasions when you choose to engage someone not currently in your sight or within earshot, just hold the person in your thoughts. Then, while focused on him or her in this way, say or think to yourself, "OK, but you are not your car." You can engage people with the slogan as you talk to them on the phone, as you watch them on television, as you listen to them on the radio, or as you otherwise encounter them nearby or far away. You can also engage people while you're involved in other activities such as taking a walk outside, drinking a cup of coffee in your kitchen, reflecting on an act of bigotry previously committed against you, or doing various household chores during each day.

Use the same discretion when engaging people with the "you are not your car" slogan that you now use when employing the bogeyman jingle and the "up a tree" metaphor. You absolutely do not have tell anyone what you are doing. However, you may in fact choose to tell certain people who appear to be open and receptive to detachment, especially if you believe detachment would be beneficial to them. In addition, on some occasions you may choose to speak the words, "OK, but you are not your car" out loud to different people who have highly inflated egos, just to tell them a few things about themselves. Be mindful, however, that whether or not you speak the slogan out loud, you do not have to convince anyone outside of you of the truth of what you're doing. You would probably not be able to convince many people anyway, no matter what you say. Just go on with your business. You do not need the agreement of others to know you are not your roles and identities. All you have to do is know it for yourself.

Just to be clear, when engaging others with the slogan "you are not your car" in the privacy of your mind, you should not do so out of fear. You engage people in this way as a matter of convenience. Engaging people out loud requires time, effort, and opportunity. When you engage them in your mind only, you have unlimited opportunities to do so, and the time required to complete each engagement is minimal. In addition, you do not have the burden of answering questions or comments you may get from the people you engage. You do not need the burden. After all, you are not trying to convince others of anything. You are engaging others only as a lighthearted but effective reminder to yourself that you are not your roles or identities.

Don't be concerned that you may not find opportunities to engage people with the slogan. All you have to do is live each day, and different opportunities will actually find you. From day to day, without any effort on your part, you will become aware of people who believe they are more valuable than others, people who say or do things to put others down, people who define themselves as victims, people who persist in judging other people, and people who are otherwise attached to the roles they play.

On the other hand, don't feel obliged to engage someone every single time an opportunity is presented. At times, you may be preoccupied with other things when an opportunity is presented, and you may not remember to act on it. At other times you may remember to engage someone, but just don't feel like doing so at that particular time. If so, that's not a problem. Undoubtedly, if you engage multiple individuals on a daily basis, you will grow much faster and more deeply on the inside than you would otherwise. But still there is no reason to overreach. Some days you may engage as many as four or five individuals or perhaps even more. On other days you may engage only one or two. Some days you may engage none. Just be comfortable with whatever each day brings. You're doing just fine if you engage others with the slogan on a regular basis.

There is no reason for you to be somber, agitated, or wary as you practice detachment. Actually, you should be cheerful, upbeat, and light of heart. It's a game. You're telling people they are not the cars they own, and they don't hear a word you're saying. Have fun with it, and know that as you're having your fun, you're protecting yourself on the inside. Most importantly, you're furthering your growth and development. You are reminding yourself that you are not the roles you play, thereby implementing this powerful truth more deeply and more completely into your life.

DAILY MEDITATIONS

In addition to engaging people with the "you are not your car" slogan, as described, you may also choose to enhance your awareness that you are not the roles you play by reading daily reflections that nurture the inner self. There are several published books available that provide a different, brief discussion on personal growth and development for each of the 365 days of the calendar year. Be careful to choose one or more books that focus on nurturing the inner self. Consider books such as *Living Life Fully's Daily Meditations, Year One* (Kindle edition), by Tom Walsh; *Daily Meditations for Practicing the Course*, by Karen Casey; *A Year of Miracles: Daily Devotions and Reflections*, by Marianne Williams; and *A Deep Breath of Life*, by Alan Cohen. The books mentioned here, ones that we enjoy and use, are offered as examples. There is much on the market from which to choose. You may also search the Internet for different websites that provide daily meditations.

Your goal is to read one daily meditation each day of the year from a book or other source you choose. If you miss a day or two, from time to time, that's no problem. Just be sure to get back to your reading as soon as possible.

You do not have to accept or believe everything you read in a particular book or on a particular website. Some things you read will speak to you strongly. Other things you read may seem wrong or irrelevant. Just accept that which sounds good and helpful to you, and leave the rest on the table. If you choose the right book or other source, you'll find much to your liking. The reading of daily meditations that focus on the inner self will nurture and support you not only in your awareness that you are not the roles you play, but also in other aspects of your life.

You now have two tools to assist you in your goal to detach from your roles and identities. Your primary tool is the slogan, "OK, but you are not your car." Your other tool is the reading of daily meditations. These tools will work only if you use them on a regular and consistent basis. And be patient: You are changing a perception of yourself that has been with you for a very long time. But if you stay the course, you will experience the lifting of a heavy burden. You will experience a strengthening on the inside that will greatly improve the quality of your life.

When you judge your value as a human being based on your roles and identities, you actually reduce the measure of yourself. No matter how great any of your roles and identities may be, who and what you truly are, are much greater. When you are attached to your roles and identities, you not only subject your sense of self-worth to the manipulation of people and things outside of you, but you also reduce yourself to something that you're not. You are much too precious as a human being to dismiss yourself in any way.

Don't Debate the Lie

As stated earlier in this book, protecting yourself from mental and emotional harm does not mean that you stop holding bigots accountable or that you stop standing up for yourself when bigots do something or say something to try to put you down. You should continue to seek remedies for wrongs committed against you. You should continue to confront bigots when they come after you. But now, when you seek remedies or take other action to confront bigots, you should, in most cases, do so without trying to prove your value as a human being. Your value as a human being is not debatable. When you try to prove your value as a human being, the result is a compromise in the integrity of your belief in human equality.

As an illustration of how you might compromise your belief, consider the following example: If your neighbor were to come to your house and call you "stupid," would you respond by gathering evidence or making different arguments to prove that you are not stupid? It is not a good idea to do that; when you get into an argument over whether or not you're stupid, you have already lost that argument no matter what you say. You would have compromised yourself by arguing against a statement that is not worthy of debate.

If you see no problem in arguing that you're not stupid, then consider this: What if your neighbor were to call you a monkey? If your neighbor were to call you a monkey, would you try to prove to your neighbor that you're not a monkey? It's probable that you won't, because when you get into an argument over whether or not you are a monkey, you have clearly gone down a path that's not in your best interest.

136

CONFRONT THE BIGOT, NOT THE LIE

Of course, when bigots attack you, you are not going to just sit there and let them run all over you. You are still going to stand up for yourself. However, when you now stand up for yourself, how will you do it? Consider, again, the example of arguing with your neighbor who calls you "stupid." If your neighbor were to call you "stupid," you should certainly confront your neighbor in some form or fashion. But you probably wouldn't accommodate this individual by trying to prove your intelligence. You should do likewise with bigots. Confront the bigots but not the lies perpetrated by bigots. Confront bigots, but let their lies dissipate in the wind.

When involved in a confrontation with a bigot, use specific comments or questions throughout the encounter to direct and keep the focus of the conversation on the bigot himself, and not on you or others who are the subjects of the bigot's attack. For example, when a bigot does something or says something to try to put you or others down, your initial response could be a statement such as, "I understand why you would say that (or do that). People do try to put others down in order to feel good about themselves." Or you might say, "Just to be sure we're on the same page, you're doing that (or saying that) in order to feel good about yourself, right?"

You certainly do not have to use the specific words offered in the above illustrations. If you choose other words, that's not a problem. If you want to be more forceful, then go ahead and be as forceful as you need to be. Use whatever words you feel are most appropriate for you, provided that you direct the focus on the bigot and the bigot's effort to feel good by putting others down.

Each act of bigotry is different. Each bigot is different. Therefore, no one can say for sure how any particular bigot will react to your saying that he or she is trying to feel good about himself or herself. However, you can and should anticipate that bigots will probably try to shift the focus back to the person or people they are demeaning. They will probably deny they are trying to make themselves feel good and insist that their disparaging statements or behaviors speak the truth. If the bigot tries to justify himself or herself in one or more of these ways as described, you would answer once again with comments or questions directing the focus back on the bigot. And thereafter, throughout the entire confrontation, you will continue to direct the focus, as you are able, back on the bigot and his motivation.

Here are some examples of how you might respond to the bigot during the confrontation after your initial response.

The bigot says, "I'm sorry if what I said offends you. But I'm speaking the truth and if the truth hurts you, that's not my problem."

You reply, "The only truth you're speaking is that you're insecure and believe you can make yourself whole by putting other people down."

The bigot says, "You're in denial. You won't admit that what I said is true."

You reply, "When you do something or say something to try to put other people down, there is no truth in it. The denial that's going on here is your refusal to take responsibility for merely trying to make yourself feel better."

The bigot says, "I am not trying to make myself feel better. That's totally ridiculous."

You reply, "If it doesn't make you feel better, then stop doing it."

The bigot says, "I am not trying to put anybody down. I don't have to. These people put themselves down by their own behavior."

You reply, "There you go again. How does that make you feel?"

The bigot says, "You're still refusing to accept the truth of what I'm saying."

You reply, "You're the one who's attacking other people. You do not define what your attack means to me. Take a look at yourself. If putting people down didn't make you feel good, you would stop it."

Again, these examples are offered for illustration. Let them be your guide, but use whatever words you feel are best suited for you, so long as you keep the focus on the bigot and his attempt to feel good about himself by putting others down.

CONFRONTING THE BIGOT WITH YOUR PERSONAL REMINDERS

Of course, when bigots come after you, you will always protect yourself on the inside by using one or more of the reminders discussed earlier: the bogeyman jingle, the "up a tree" metaphor, or the "you are not your car" slogan. While these reminders were designed primarily for your own use, in some cases they may work just fine in confrontations with those who try to put you down.

Notice that each of the three reminders that you use to protect yourself on the inside satisfies the requirement that you should confront bigots and not the lie perpetrated by them. The bogeyman jingle is a reminder that bigots believe in the illusion that some people are more valuable than others. The "up a tree" metaphor reminds you that bigots are compromised in their ability to harm others on the inside. The "you are not your car" slogan reminds you that bigots wrongly believe people *are* the roles they play.

Whether you speak one or more of your reminders out loud to a bigot in your confrontation with him is your decision to make on a case-by-case basis. If you do choose to use a reminder in a particular confrontation, just be careful that you do not get caught up in a debate trying to justify your reminder to bigots. You are not going to persuade bigots no matter what you say and you do not need their agreement to protect yourself from mental and emotional harm.

DISREGARDING THE BIGOTRY OF OTHERS

Perhaps you feel an obligation to confront bigots openly and directly every time they commit acts of bigotry against you or against others in your presence. Surely, you want to persist in standing up for yourself and others for your personal protection and for the betterment of our society. But there are times when direct confrontation is not the best or most appropriate response to a given situation.

Confronting bigots each and every time they commit an act of bigotry against you or others, no matter how subtle or ambiguous the act may be, would be an awesome burden to bear, and would likely give you the reputation of someone who is obsessed with being a victim. This would likely diminish your credibility with others. With some subtle acts of bigotry, it's just not worth the effort to engage bigots in confrontation.

In addition, sometimes bigots are threatened when they notice that you are interacting with others as though you are inferior to no one. They often respond by making bigoted comments for the sole purpose of reminding you of your status in society as they see it. They don't speak it outright, but clearly their message is this: "Don't you know you're black?" or "Don't you know you're Mexican?" or "Don't you know you're Puerto Rican?" and so forth and so on. They want and expect you to defend yourself against their bigoted comments because it gives them gratification when you do. Be careful that you do not accommodate bigots in this devious behavior. Sometimes, but certainly not always, the best response in a situation as described is to disregard the bigoted behavior altogether, especially if you're in the company of supportive people who are aware of what the bigots are trying to accomplish. Sometimes your best answer is to let a bigot dance in the wind, all alone.

Further, in selected cases, you may choose to disregard particular acts of bigotry as a specific way of providing feedback to bigots. For example, if a bigot commits a subtle or ambiguous act of bigotry against you or others in an ongoing conversation, you could simply not comment on what the bigot has said and allow the conversation to move on. You could even direct the conversation to other matters or withdraw or walk away from the conversation altogether. In some cases, when you disregard an act of bigotry, you give bigots indirect but powerful feedback that their lies are totally without merit and not even worthy of a response. Of course, if a bigot persists with such bigoted behavior, after you have disregarded it, everything changes. At that point you may choose to confront him or her directly.

Intentionally disregarding the bigotry of others for your benefit is best suited for those subtle incidents of bigotry that do not affect you on the inside in a significant way. If an incident of bigotry angers you or otherwise disturbs you to the extent that you feel you must speak out, then go ahead and speak out. Also, you certainly would not disregard an act of bigotry when you need to speak out in public to protect your reputation or standing among others. For example, sometimes you may need to confront bigots openly and directly so that employees you supervise or colleagues in your community or profession do not get the impression that you lack the courage to stand up for yourself.

Whether you disregard a particular act of bigotry in your encounters with bigots is entirely up to you. Just be mindful that as you continue your journey that disregarding the bigotry of others is an *alternative* to direct confrontation that may work well in certain situations.

EXCEPTIONS TO THE "DON'T DEBATE THE LIE" RULE

Confronting the bigot but not the lie is an important discipline in the overall process of protecting yourself on the inside. However, there are some very necessary and significant exceptions to this rule.

The "Don't Debate the Lie" rule does not apply to efforts, programs, conversations, or other initiatives used to destroy bigotry and prejudice in the general population. As a society, we must certainly continue to teach people bigotry is wrong. We must continue to explain why there are disparities among different groups in our society in housing, education, and income. We must continue to teach the message that everyone is entitled to be treated with dignity and respect, without regard to the roles, identities, or labels we assign each other. There is an enormous distinction between teaching people about bigotry for the purpose of building a better society and trying to prove your value as a human being. Improving society is essential. Trying to prove your value as a human is a mistake because there is nothing to prove in this regard in the first place.

Another exception to the "Don't Debate the Lie" rule arises out of the understanding that not everyone who says something or does something that hurts you on the inside is motivated to harm you. Sometimes individuals will commit acts of bigotry against you or others and not realize their conduct is offensive. When confronted about their behavior, these individuals may ask you to help them understand. Or you may discern without prompting from them that they do not understand. You will have to decide for yourself on a case-by-case basis whether people genuinely do not understand or are simply trying to manipulate you further. Just make the best decision that you can and respond accordingly. If individuals you encounter truly do not understand their conduct is offensive, and they intend no harm, talk to them about their harmful behavior and help them to understand.

In addition, if want to excuse yourself from applying the "Don't Debate the Lie" rule in any given situation, then go ahead and excuse yourself. Perhaps you're having a bad day. Perhaps you're involved in a particularly feisty confrontation. Perhaps you cannot even articulate the reason, but you just don't feel like applying the rule on a particular occasion. If this happens to you, this is not a problem. Just keep this important rule in the back of your mind and get back to using it as soon as you can.

Applying "Don't Debate the Lie" does not mean you will stop doing the important things in your life that you are currently doing. You will continue your efforts to eliminate all forms of bigotry and prejudice that exist in our society. You will continue to seek remedies when bigots assault you or deny you your legal and human rights. You will continue to hold bigots accountable. You will continue to confront bigots as forcefully as you choose. You will continue to use all components of this strategy to improve the quality of your life.

Contrary to what may be the initial impression of some, "Don't Debate the Lie" is not a concession but an aggressive step forward. When you refuse to debate the lie, you protect yourself in the integrity of your belief that you are a valuable human being. After all, you would not try to prove you're not stupid. You would not try to prove you're not a monkey. Likewise, do not compromise yourself by offering proof of your value as a human being. There is nothing to prove. Your value as a human being depends on nothing, and it is yours without conditions. No person, thing, or occurrence can take your value away from you.

Abandon All Hostilities

To PROTECT YOURSELF on the inside from the bigotry and prejudice of others, you must also give up any anger, hatred, resentment, or other animosity you harbor against individuals or groups for wrongs committed against you. Contrary to what some may believe, when you harbor hostilities against others you do great harm to yourself.

Harboring of hostilities results in agitation for the person who's doing the harboring. After all, when you hate, resent, or hold anger against others, you don't go around dancing and singing with a joyful heart about it. Instead, you are unsettled or otherwise burdened with negative thoughts and emotions. Clearly, you would be in a much better mood and live a more peaceful life if you did not have such negativity dwelling within.

Your hostilities harm you in other ways as well. They take time and energy that you could otherwise use in the pursuit of important goals. Hostilities penetrate deeply into your whole being and negatively affect all aspects of your life. They guarantee the negative presence of bigots in your life until you finally awaken to the truth of what's really going on in your life.

In addition, when you harbor hostilities, some people will find it uncomfortable to be around you. After all, who wants to be around someone who is always angry and resentful? Further, some people may become distrustful of you out of fear that you if you have hostilities against others, you might one day develop hostilities against them as well. If people mistrust you or don't want to be around you because of your anger, hatred, or resentment, they are not likely to hire you for jobs or assist you with other opportunities.

You have to let your hostilities go. Do not be misled by the argument that it is the responsibility of bigots to stop any hostilities that you may be harboring. Perhaps you have entertained the thought or heard others say that since bigots caused your hostilities, they should make them go away. But remember that bigots are not inclined to cooperate with you in this regard. Waiting for people or things outside of you to change before you take action to protect yourself only hurts you. Only you can take action to relinquish your hostilities.

You might have other thoughts or hear other arguments that suggest that others should take responsibility for your hostilities. Just be mindful that giving up your hostilities is not a concession to bigots, but a powerful action in support of your personal well-being and liberation from the bigots and bigotry that you encounter in your life. If *you* do not take action to abandon your hostilities, it's not going to happen. No one else can do it for you.

To be clear, letting go of your hostilities does not mean you should deny them. If you feel anger, hatred, or resentment, then that's what you feel. Letting go of your hostilities is not about denial. It is about going to a place mentally and emotionally where you do not have hostilities. It is about going to a place where there are no hostilities to deny.

Your awareness that your hostilities harm you, together with your commitment to make a change in your life, will put you on the path to unburden yourself and will continue to sustain you throughout your journey. You will also find relief from your hostilities by implementing all of the other components of the strategy. When you recognize all bigotry as a lie, when you know bigots act out of their own fear and feelings of inadequacy, and when you understand and appreciate that you are not the roles and identities you play, the anger, hatred, resentment, and other animosity you harbor against bigots will diminish tremendously, if not dissolve altogether.

Another practice that you might choose to help you abandon your hostilities is to pray for the bigots you encounter. If you do not believe in prayer, you could just offer best wishes to them. In the beginning, your prayers or best wishes may not be heartfelt. However, over a period of time, what you say or think may become sincere. When you pray or offer best wishes to others in earnest, your hostility against them will diminish.

Always keep in mind that when you harbor hostilities against others, you are only harming yourself. With this very important understanding in place as your foundation, use other practices and principles available to you to support you on your path to liberation.

SUMMARY

UNTIL THE DAY comes when everyone is treated with dignity and respect, what will you do in the meantime to protect yourself from loss of self-esteem and other mental and emotional harm caused by bigotry and other disrespect you encounter? If you experience bigotry and prejudice and do nothing to protect yourself on the inside, the ensuing mental and emotional harm, especially the loss of self-esteem, will deny you equal opportunity and impair the overall quality of your life.

You can protect yourself from mental and emotional harm caused by bigotry and other disrespect by implementing the five-component strategy recommended in this book. The components of this strategy are: (1) recognize all bigotry as a lie, (2) awaken to the bigot's motivation, (3) detach from your roles and identities, (4) don't debate the lie, and (5) abandon all hostilities.

This book provides understanding of and perspectives about each component of the strategy. What you must do now is use the tools that we also provided to make these understandings and perspectives come alive in your life. The powerful liberating truths with which you have now been armed will mean little or nothing if you do not implement them. Reading and comprehending this book are not the last things you must do to protect yourself. They are just the beginning steps.

The task ahead is not daunting or imposing. Actually, your path is quite simple, but it is certainly not always easy, because at times much patience and discipline are required. Overall, your journey forward can be both lighthearted but very effective, if you choose to make it so.

Everything you must do to protect yourself on the inside breaks down into five basic practices.

The Bogeyman Jingle

Sing the bogeyman jingle one or more times to yourself whenever someone commits an act of bigotry against you or whenever you feel hurt, belittled, bothered, intimidated or threatened in any way by bigotry or prejudice against you.

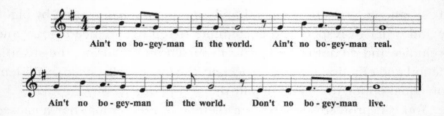

Ain't no bo-gey-man in the world. Ain't no bo-gey-man real.

Ain't no bo-gey-man in the world. Don't no bo-gey-man live.

Sing the bogeyman jingle predominantly to yourself because the jingle is not for bigots, but instead it is for you and your protection. However, if you find yourself at times singing the jingle out loud, that's OK. Sometimes you might feel compelled to sing it out loud even to bigots just to let them know what's going on with you. Also, at different times, as opportunities present themselves, you may join with others in singing the jingle out loud to support each other against the harmful attitudes and behavior of others.

Without question, some people have more material wealth than others. Some are gifted with talent that others do not have. Some may be regarded as contributing more to the benefit of humankind than others. Some achieve more than others. Some people have benefits and privileges denied to others based on social status or standing. But absolutely no one is more valuable as a human being than anyone else in the world. Indeed, the very idea itself that some people are more valuable than others as human beings is an illusion.

Every act of bigotry against you, no matter what kind, states or implies that you are inferior because you do not meet certain standards or expectations. Undeniably, standards and expectations are important, but your failure to meet certain standards or expectations does not render you inferior. Contrary to what many believe, standards and expectations are totally irrelevant to your value as a human being. Accordingly, whenever you encounter bigotry or prejudice, the first thing you must do is put aside that part of the encounter that says or implies that you do not meet certain standards or expectations. At the time of the attack against you or at the moment you are feeling diminished in any way by the bigotry or prejudice of others, simply use the bogeyman jingle to remind yourself that you are not inferior, because the idea itself that some people are more valuable than others is an illusion.

The belief that some people are more valuable than others as human beings is no different from the belief that the bogeyman is real. Both beliefs presume the existence of something that does not exist. Accordingly, it is fitting to use the bogeyman analogy to protect yourself on the inside from the bigotry and prejudice you experience.

The bogeyman jingle is your constant reminder that there is no such thing as inequality in human value. It is your reminder that you are a valuable human being, just as valuable as anyone and everyone else in the world, and no person, people, thing, or occurrence can take your value away from you.

"Up a Tree" Reminder

Whenever bigots commit acts of bigotry against you or whenever you feel intimidated, frightened, angered, belittled, or otherwise bothered in any way by bigots, just say or think to yourself, "He's up a tree" or "She's up a tree." As you are able, use your imagination to actually envision a bigot up a tree, clinging there in fear and anxiety. And when you have that bigot firmly in place in the tree in your imagination, try to talk him or her down, also in the privacy of your mind.

> *Hey, [Sue or Jim]. Come down out of that tree.*
> *And stop throwing those rocks,*
> *you could hurt somebody.*
> *You don't have to throw rocks at other people*
> *to feel good about yourself; you never did.*
> *So stop throwing those rocks*
> *And come down out of that tree.*

The "up a tree" mental exercise is your reminder that the bigot is not what he or she pretends to be. In truth, the bigot is the bully on the playground. Bigots are not as strong and secure on the inside as they pretend. Instead, they are filled with fear and feelings of inadequacy. They attack others in an effort to feel good about themselves. They wrongly believe their value as a human being depend on their ability to distinguish themselves as worthy by putting others down.

Bigots can harm you mentally and emotionally only if they have some measure of credibility with you. When you understand and appreciate they are weak and insecure on the inside, their credibility is diminished, if not destroyed altogether. Their mental and emotional authority over you is severely compromised. After all, they are claiming you are inferior when they themselves are struggling with their own sense of self-worth.

Bigots will not stop in their efforts to put you down and deny you your rights and privileges. Therefore, you must continue to stand up for yourself against these assaults whenever they occur. But now that you see clearly through the false persona of bigots you have enormous protection against the mental and emotional harm they otherwise would inflict upon you.

OK, But You Are Not Your Car

At different times during the day, when you find yourself feeling particularly attached to one or more of the various roles you play in life, say to yourself, "OK, but you are not your car." In addition, say this same catchphrase to yourself concerning others, when you notice them being especially caught up in the illusion that they are the roles they play. When you use the "you are not your car" catchphrase on a persistent basis in the manner described, you strengthen yourself on the inside against any negative judgment regarding your value as a human being.

The only way anyone, including you, can judge you as inferior as a human being is by finding fault with one or more of your roles or identities. Certainly, you have little or no control over the thoughts or beliefs of others. However, for you personally, if you are judging yourself as inferior in any way or having doubts about your value as a human being, just stop assessing your value as a human being based on your roles and identities.

You are not your race, gender, occupation, economic status, place of birth, or any of the other roles and identities that may be used to describe you. Beneath all of it, you are a valuable human being, and this valuable human being residing within you is who and what you truly are.

When you detach from your roles and identities, you can see more clearly that any negative judgment against your roles and identities is *not* negative judgment against you. Negative judgment regarding your roles and identities will no longer reach you because who and what you are lives safely within.

Your roles and identities operate in your life in the same way you use your car. Surely, your car is important to you as a means of transportation. Your car gives you access to different people and places. However, no matter how valuable your car may be, you are *not* your car. It is likewise with your roles and identities. Your roles and identities may be very important personal attributes that you use to live your life. But no matter how valuable (or detrimental) your roles and identities may be, you are *not* your roles and identities.

When you detach from your roles and identities, you strengthen yourself on the inside against any and all bigotry and prejudice against you. Use the "you are not your car" catchphrase to assist you in implementing detachment more fully into your life. In addition, read daily meditations that nurture the inner self. You will find such mediations in published books and on different websites on the Internet.

Don't Debate the Lie

You are a valuable human being, just as valuable as anyone and everyone else in the world, and no person, people, thing, or occurrence can take your value away from you. This fundamental truth about your value as a human being is not debatable. To debate it is to compromise the integrity of your belief about who and what you are. Therefore, do not try to prove your value as a human being to yourself or to anyone else in the world. When you encounter bigotry and prejudice, make every effort to confront the bigot without confronting the lie perpetrated by the bigot. Confront the bigot, and let the lie dissipate in the wind.

For sure, there are some very important exceptions to this "don't debate the lie" rule. In those situations when you must debate the lie, go ahead and debate it. But keep in mind that your value as a human being is already firmly and irrevocably established. There is no greater proof of this truth than your birth into the world.

Abandon All Hostilities

Mental and emotional liberation from bigotry, prejudice, discrimination, bullying, or other disrespect you have suffered will not happen until you let go of any hostilities you harbor against the individuals and groups who perpetrated wrongs against you. Let go of any anger, resentment, hatred, or other animosity that you may be feeling.

Your hostilities against others will greatly diminish as you employ the different components of the strategy discussed in this book. In addition, you may choose to use other tools as well. For example, you may find it helpful to pray for bigots. If praying doesn't work for you, perhaps you could wish them a life of peace and love as they continue their life journey.

Your intellectual comprehension of this overall strategy is clearly the first step in your mental and emotional liberation from the harmful conduct of others. But much of the actual growth and development necessary for your liberation will occur from this day forward as you encounter bigotry and prejudice from your new perspective and witness firsthand the specific ways in which the bigoted behavior and attitudes of others do not negatively impact you as they did before. The disparaging treatment you experience and your interaction with the people who perpetrate this harm are the instruments of your personal growth.

Use the world as your workshop. Demeaning experiences and bigoted people, though difficult and painful, are also opportunities for your advancement. When you see the world as your workshop, you are more likely than not to be open and receptive to growth opportunities. Negative people and negative occurrences will not have the same influence over you.

Be mindful that the understandings, perspectives, and tools you have been provided are effective only if you use them as recommended on a regular basis. Ultimately, you and you alone can determine the depth and pace of your liberation. Be patient. Be true. And you will greatly improve the quality of your life. Nothing can stop you.

Afterword

(Eliminating Bigotry Altogether)
By Roger

⎯⎯⎯⎯⎯⎯⎯ ⌣ ⎯⎯⎯⎯⎯⎯⎯

WHEN NICOLE AND I introduce others to the strategy of *Withstanding the Lie,* we tell them up front that we are not offering an overall solution to the problem of bigotry in our society. We clearly state that we are recommending a strategy that people can use to protect themselves from mental and emotional harm caused by bigotry and other insolent attitudes and behavior until that day when everyone is treated with dignity and respect. Yet, some who want to hear our message still want to know what we believe about eliminating bigotry altogether.

As you might expect, everything that Nicole and I believe about eliminating bigotry comprises an enormous discussion that would be much too vast and weighty to include as supplemental matter in this book. However, I will offer a brief statement on what we believe society can do to improve on what is currently being done to combat bigotry.

Of course, Nicole and I have different life experiences and personalities. Thus we do not necessarily have the same perspective on each and every detail regarding a solution to bigotry. But our fundamental beliefs on eliminating all bigotry and prejudice in our society are the same.

STRONG PUBLIC POLICY AGAINST BIGOTRY AND PREJUDICE

Nicole and I believe that dignity and respect for everyone will never be realized in our society without a strong public policy against bigotry and prejudice, much stronger than the policy currently in place. Political

leaders, government appointees, public providers, public employers, religious leaders, actors, musicians, athletes, and other public figures who
have the capacity to influence public opinion must remind the public
periodically that bigotry and prejudice have no place in our society and
that everyone should be treated with dignity and respect. Public figures
must also speak out denouncing specific incidents of bigotry and prejudice when it is permissible and appropriate for them to do so.

However, Nicole and I do not believe public figures should be *required*
by law or regulations to speak out against bigotry and prejudice. Instead,
civil-rights advocates and other concerned citizens should use different
measures of persuasion to encourage public-figure participation. These
measures may include protest activities, boycotts, and signed petitions
against those who do not make appropriate public statements. Specific
requests addressed to those who fail to speak out would be made public.
The names of those who speak out and the names of those who remain
silent would also be made public.

Civil-rights advocates and other concerned citizens would pay special attention to candidates who are campaigning for election or reelec-
tion to local, state, or federal office. Different candidates would be asked
specifically to make a commitment to speak out publicly against bigotry
and prejudice if elected or reelected. Obviously, the incentive for the
candidates is that if they do not make the commitment or subsequently
fail to keep the commitment, they would expose themselves to the risk
of losing the support of a significant number of voters.

Of course, no manner of persuasion will convince *all* public figures
to speak out against bigotry and prejudice as one might hope. But that's
not a deal breaker. Substantial participation by public figures is sufficient. With regard to defining "substantial participation," we say, "You'll
know it when you see it."

A strong public policy against bigotry and prejudice, as I have described, will persuade many in our society who have gone astray to give
up their bigoted attitudes and behavior. Of course, some who harbor
bigotry and prejudice will never be persuaded to change. But they too,

like all humans, will each in his or her own time submit to the experience called death. And when they die, their bigoted beliefs are more likely than not to die with them, and not be passed from one generation to the next if our leaders and public figures actively promote and exemplify dignity and respect for all.

STRONG POLITICAL PARTICIPATION

Surely, a necessary component of an effective public policy against bigotry and prejudice is the strong political participation of people who suffer bigotry and prejudice and others who support them. People who care about dignity and respect must vote in the democratic process to elect political leaders at the local, state, and national levels who are committed to speaking out publicly against bigotry and prejudice. Of course, leaders must also be committed to work with others to enact, maintain, and enforce laws that prohibit discrimination and address existing inequities.

To make strong political participation as described a reality, civil-rights advocates and other concerned citizens must work continuously to persuade and remind affected people, and their supporters, to register and vote in each and every election for the candidates who will best serve their interests. The message to voters is simple. Sometimes you may feel that your vote doesn't make a difference. Well, that's precisely how bigots want you to feel. Bigots know how powerful your vote is. They understand that it's a gift to them when you stay home. Don't let anybody fool you. When you do not register and vote for the person you believe is the best candidate, you make it easier for a candidate who doesn't represent your values to get elected. By not voting, you are actually voting for someone who may want to harm you or at least do nothing to protect you when others try to take away your rights and privileges.

At times, you may see no tangible benefits of your vote and feel you're being "smart" by staying home and not voting at all. You have to remember that progress takes time. Also, if you stay home, and let the wrong people get elected, making progress will not be your only concern. The politicians who get elected because you stayed home may try to take away the progress that has already been made by hard sacrifices of the past.

Indeed, voting in every election may be inconvenient and in some situations difficult. But that's no excuse. Understand that concerned people are working hard to improve the voting process. But still there is no excuse for not doing what it takes right now to register and vote. Get out there and register and vote. You owe it to yourself, you owe it to those who have sacrificed in the past, and you owe it to the generations of the future.

Addressing Specific Acts of Bigotry and Other Inequities

Nicole and I believe black people should not be the only ones participating in protest activities and other initiatives to stop discrimination against black people. White people and other nonblack people, of whatever race, creed, or religion, should be equally involved. Initiatives to confront bigotry against certain religious groups are not the sole responsibility of the individuals in the groups under attack. Full and active participation to stop this bigotry should also come from others in the general population. Initiatives to stop discrimination against women should have the active participation of both men and women. Protest activities and other initiatives to address any and all acts of bigotry and prejudice in our society should have the participation of a diversity of people working together to achieve the common goal of dignity and respect for all.

Do not think that diversity of people in civil-rights initiatives is a matter only of a personal preference. It is an important way of doing things that gets good results. For example, in the United States, the abolition of slavery, the elimination of laws requiring segregation and discrimination, and the enactment of the Civil Rights Act of 1964 prohibiting racial discrimination in employment and public accommodations were accomplished not by the acts of black people alone, but by the courageous acts of both blacks and whites in the interest of justice. For sure, the protest activities of blacks alone would have resulted in a much different scenario in race relations in the United States than what our country in fact experienced.

Nicole and I are convinced that no bigotry in the United States against any particular group will prevail if an overwhelming number of people, inside and outside that group, speak out for justice and equality. But diversity in civil-rights initiatives will not just suddenly appear or happen on its own. It will happen only if action is taken to make it happen. Thus, civil-rights advocates and others who organize or promote civil-rights initiatives must incorporate a strategy to invite and encourage people from the general population—people who do not themselves experience the bigotry being addressed—to get involved in those civil-rights activities. Invite and encourage others to participate fully, including in leadership roles. Make the case that bigotry against any particular group is also an assault against us all. Lack of dignity and respect, even if only against "others," breaks down the strength and integrity of our entire society.

Notice that misguided people often portray certain civil-rights initiatives as conflict between different groups, such as conflict between blacks and whites, conflict between males and females, conflict between the LGBTQ+ community and the general public, conflict between Muslims and Christians, and so on. Bigots in particular believe they can undermine or diminish civil-rights efforts by portraying such efforts as the selfish interest of particular groups. Therefore, civil-rights advocates must be careful in the way they frame, label, or define what they are trying to accomplish. Whenever possible, they should use language, slogans, and labels that do not only suggest the interest of a particular group. Let the public know the subject matter is also an assault against society as a whole. Ultimately however, if people of all different races, religions, and ethnic identities participate together in confronting bigotry and prejudice, the bigot would be diminished in his ability to mislead the public.

Whether civil-rights advocates and other concerned citizens pursue a path such as the one recommended by Nicole and me *or* take a different course of action altogether, the elimination of substantially all bigotry and prejudice from our society will only occur, if at all, after generations into the future. In all likelihood, complete justice and fairness for many is still a long time coming. However, despite the bigotry and prejudice you encounter now, society's delay in providing dignity and respect for all is not the final word on the quality of life available to you right now.

Some people today who suffer bigotry and prejudice in our society actually feel complete in the way they live their lives, and they truly live their lives with a great sense of satisfaction and inner peace. Others who experience bigotry and prejudice can have that same level of quality in their lives if they change the way they perceive and understand themselves and others in the world.